CONCISE HISTORY OF CATHOLICISM

By

Marian McKenna

Manhattanville College of the Sacred Heart

1962

LITTLEFIELD, ADAMS & COMPANY

Paterson 1, New Jersey

Imprimatur ✠ FRANCIS CARDINAL SPELLMAN,
Archbishop of New York

NIHIL OBSTAT

James A. Reynolds, Ph.D., *Censor Librorum*
July 26, 1961

1962 Edition

LITTLEFIELD, ADAMS & COMPANY

This book contains the text, only, of a larger volume entitled, *Pictorial History of Catholicism,* published and copyrighted by Philosophical Library, Inc., 1962.

Library of Congress Catalog Card No. 61-12622

Printed in the United States of America

Contents

63068

I

The Apostolic Age

The historian, Preserved Smith, has introduced the subject of Christianity in words that will bear quoting to begin the story of the Catholic Church. He wrote that Christianity was immaculately conceived in the heart of a Galilean carpenter and born with words of beauty and power such as no other man ever spoke. It inherited from its background Jewish monotheism and Hebrew scripture. It was enriched by Paul with the current mysteries of salvation by sacramental rite. It decked itself in the white robes of Greek philosophy and created a pantheon of saints to replace the former Roman gods. It became the chaplain and finally the heir of the Roman empire, building its church upon the immovable rock of the eternal city, conquering and taming the barbarians, asserting a dominion without bounds of space or time.[1]

The great facts of all Christian history are the birth of Christ, His life of teaching and good example while on earth, His passion and crucifixion, and the triumph of His resurrection. Ten days after His ascension into Heaven came the first Christian Pentecost, next to the crucifixion and resurrection the most momentous event for the Catholic believer. The first followers of Christ were Jews, orthodox in their observance of the Mosaic law. They were not even called Christians as yet, for many of them had at first looked upon their Master as

3

king of the Jews; then they looked to an early second coming of the Messiah to judge all men, reward the good and punish the wicked. To those first believers, Christ had spoken of his universal mission, commanding his disciples: "Going therefore, teach ye all nations, baptizing them in the name of the Father and of the Son and of the Holy Ghost." As yet, the concept expressed by the word *Catholic,* borrowed at a later time from the Greek, was, at the most, latent in their minds.[2]

In the Cenacle of Jerusalem was gathered the small community of Christians around Mary, the Mother of Jesus. There was Simon Peter, the headstrong, passionate fisherman to whom Christ had given the commission in two of the four Gospels, "Feed my sheep" and "Feed my lambs," thus foreshadowing the establishment of the Church. St. Matthew records that Christ used the Aramaic form of the Apostle's name to make known His choice of Simon as head of the Church when He said, "Thou art Peter, and upon this rock I will build my Church, and the gates of hell shall not prevail against it." To Peter, the rock, had been committed the keys of the Kingdom. With Peter, who became the spokesman for the others when any crisis arose, were ten others of the original twelve Apostles, and one Matthias, recently chosen by lot to replace the traitor, Judas. The title "apostle" was not confined to the first twelve (of old a sacred number which had been determined by Jesus). It was also conferred on St. Paul and his companions, Barnabas and Silas. Right down to the Middle Ages, messengers of the Gospel were called "Apostles." Other disciples made a total of about a hundred and twenty people who were witnesses on the day of Pentecost to the outpouring of what the theologians call divine grace on that little group. The descent of the Holy Spirit on the twelve

Apostles was symbolized by parted tongues of fire. The amazed by-standers, from many scattered regions of the Near East, heard the new faith preached in all their different languages by this group of Galilean provincials. When Peter, whose primacy seemed already recognized by his brethren, addressed the crowd in the first sermon preached to the infant Church, many who had at first mocked listened respectfully. By the day's end about three thousand converts were baptized, thus becoming the first fruits of a missionary work that still continues.

Not even the burning words of Peter, who spoke in rustic accents as a Jew to Jews, hinted this early at the world-wide Christian mission, which would address itself "equally to Jews and Gentiles, freemen and slaves, intellectual Hellenists, practical, empire-governing Romans, and the obscure, anonymous millions" of all ages. Only gradually, and after much argument and friction among brethren would the idea of Catholicity, that is, universality, come to dominate the minds of the early Jewish Christians and set the pattern for their future work. From the second century onward the word "Catholic" was in general use by Christian writers.[3]

The story of the spread of Christianity into the world, then, begins with the descent of the Holy Ghost on Pentecost. Very quickly these first disciples—"Jews, devout men out of every nation under Heaven"— must have spread the news of "the wonder of Tongues" far and wide. Peter, who was the leading personality of the young Christian community, preached at the Council of Jerusalem (49 A.D.), where the principle was admitted that Gentile converts, along with Jews, were admissible to the Church without going through a probationary stage of Judaic practice. including circumcision. It was Peter who, inspired by the Holy Ghost, baptized the first Gentile. He also preached at Antioch, whose first bishop he was, at Corinth and Rome, where he was to become that city's first bishop. His presence was to make Rome the center of Christendom. It was here in this city, during the course of Nero's persecution of the Christians between 64 and 67 that Peter was crucified, his head downward to distinguish his humble death from the crucifixion of his Lord. Michelangelo portrayed his martyrdom in the paintings now displayed in the chapel of the Vatican. At a very early period Peter was honored at Rome as a local saint; according to the customs of Christian antiquity this was possible only if he was buried in Rome. Excavations under the basilica of St. Peter's since 1940 have yielded archaeological evidence of the Apostle's burial under the confessional.

The great scarcity of documentary evidence for the history of the Church from the Apostolic age to the beginning of the third century makes it impossible to trace in any really accurate detail the steps by which episcopal government, that is, each bishop ruling his own diocese, replaced the government of the Church by the Apostles themselves. We mark the beginnings of it in the pastoral epistles of St. Paul. The apostolic college remains in the College of Bishops. Over them is one of their own number—the Bishop of Rome, the successor of St. Peter, as bishop of the See in which St. Peter died and to which he left his privileges. Communications were difficult in this age of persecution but the primacy of the Bishop of Rome was everywhere acknowledged as well as claimed. As head over the whole Church, the Bishop of Rome later acquired the exclusive title of Pope.

In this early period, three bishops of Antioch, Alexandria and Rome headed the hierarchy of the Church and were later given the title "Patriarch." By the fifth century, Constantinople and Jerusalem had attained the patriarchal rank.

Historians of the Catholic Church have found several themes which run through the whole of Catholic history like threads. There is, first, the Church's awareness of a missionary vocation—the task to spread the Faith to all the corners of the earth. Second, there is the tradition of martyrdom, which originated with the earliest experience of Christ's followers. A survey of Church history over two thousand years reveals that, when we use the term "martyr" in its broadest sense to embrace the higher kinds of holy living, suffering in some form or another has always been a part of the witness which sanctity bears to the Faith. A third theme we shall view is the achievements through the early period of the Church's history of those we call the Christian apologists. A fourth theme is the Church's continuing struggle against heresy. As the mystical Body of Christ, which is His Church, grows in membership and influence, the attack on what we call heresy is broadened. Heresy is a word which theologians have taken from the Greek verb meaning "to choose." A heretic is one who chooses among the articles of faith, accepting those he likes and rejecting others, or substituting for them his own opinions. These various aspects of the life and work of the early Church formed a pattern which has lasted for twenty centuries. In this pattern we can further perceive the three phases or stages through which the orderly minds of theologians see the Church advancing toward the ends set by her Founder. Thus we have the Church Militant, fighting against sin, error and scandal; the Church Suffering, a sequel to the first stage and also contemporary with it; and lastly, the Church Triumphant, the faithful enjoying the presence of God in Heaven.

When the Roman Emperor Claudius issued his decree forbidding Jewish worship in Rome, Christians fell under this ban since they were still considered a Jewish sect. Oppression of the Christians in Judea, under Herod Agrippa, resulted in the execution of St. James the Great, who never left Judea. St. James the Less, though strongly attached to the Jewish tradition, was sentenced to death on a charge of having violated the Law of Moses. St. Peter was imprisoned in Jerusalem, but after his miraculous escape he fled to Rome. Among those who left Jerusalem was St. John the Evangelist, who went to Asia Minor, where he wrote the Fourth Gospel and Epistles. During a later persecution he was exiled to the island of Patmos, where he wrote the Apocalypse, a revelation of the things that were, are and shall be. Four years later (100 A.D.), St. John died, probably at Ephesus.

The keynote of the new mode of life and thought, which we know as Christianity, was simply charity or love, the twofold love of God and His creature, man, the law which Christ preached as forming the two great commandments. St. John struck this keynote when he wrote, "God is love." And to the followers of the divine Master, he wrote: "Dearly beloved, love one another." When one of them asked why he always returned to this precept, St. John answered: "It is the precept of the Savior; if one observes it, that is enough."

Of the other Apostles we know very little. Tradition allots Scythia and even Russia to the missionary work of St. Andrew; Ethiopia to St. Matthew; Phrygia to

St. Philip; and Edessa to St. Thaddeus. St. Mark may have carried the word of the Gospel to Alexandria in Egypt, where there was a large Jewish colony.

From the earliest beginnings, the story of the Catholic Church was to be largely a record of missionary activity, and first rank among the apostolic missionaries belongs to St. Paul. Born as Saul, in Tarsus, Cilicia, he was an orthodox Jew who acquired Roman citizenship by virtue of his birth in a colony of the Roman Empire. After studying law he became a rabbi in Jerusalem, where he witnessed the death of St. Stephen, stoned by a fanatical mob. "Saul," says the Book of Acts, "was consenting unto his death." The account of the persecutor Saul's journey to Damascus to arrest disciples of Christ, of his temporary blindness, and of the voice from Heaven rebuking him for his ruthless and misguided zeal in hunting down Christians, is a familiar story. After three days of blindness, prayer and fasting, Saul received his sight through the mediation of Ananius, a Christian in Damascus. From then on Paul, as he was later known, becomes the Apostle of the Gentiles, preacher, theologian, founder of churches, mystic and missionary. Peter was the first disciple to baptize a Gentile, but it was Paul who helped him convert the Apostles to the doctrine that Jesus had come to earth to redeem all men, not just the Jews.

At Jerusalem Paul met Peter. When the Jews forced him to leave, Paul embarked on those remarkable journeys that were to take him, during a quarter of a century, over thousands of miles. Amid frequent sufferings and hardships he labored unceasingly, preaching, writing, constantly emphasizing the divinity of Christ and his resurrection. On Cyprus, he converted the Roman proconsul. Throughout Turkey, Greece, Macedonia and Antioch he continued his missionary journeys until he came once again to Jerusalem, where he narrowly escaped death at the hands of a mob, saved only by his Roman citizenship. After more travel, vicissitudes, controversy and imprisonment, he came at last to Rome, where he was beheaded during the persecution of Nero, thus dying a martyr for the Christian Faith he had once helped to persecute. In his own words, he had fought the good fight, finished the course, and kept the faith.

Of details concerning the life and religious practice of the early Christians, whether in Europe or Asia, we know only too little. Since most Christians in the early part of the first century belonged to the Jewish religion, they continued to observe such practices as attendance at Temple and observance of the Sabbath. To these they added the Christian ceremony, the breaking of bread, or the Eucharistic feast. In his first apology, Justin gives us a vivid account of the celebration of the Lord's Supper. The book of the Acts of the Apostles tells us of a voluntary community of goods in the Church in Jerusalem. The more fervent converts, it seems, pooled their money and labor for the general welfare, much as did the monks and nuns of a later time. That there was a high level of altruism and what is now called charitable work, we know from the constant references to almsgiving and from the fact that deacons had to be appointed for this work of serving the poor, so that the fully ordained priesthood might be left free for strictly religious duties. We know, too, that a common comment among pagan observers, looking on in bewilderment and hostility at the new religion, was: "See how these Christians love one another."

The word *martyr*, of Greek origin, means simply a witness, but in Church history the term is limited to the supreme and ultimate witness any human being can give, namely, testimony sealed with his lifeblood. The first persecution of Christians may be said to have started with the martyrdom of St. Stephen, a Greek Jew and one of the seven deacons first chosen to help the Apostles in administering the temporal affairs of the early Church community. In one of his many debates with the Jews, Stephen promised that Jesus of Nazareth would change the customs Moses had established. Before the Sanhedrin (the Supreme Council), Stephen launched into a violent attack on the Jews, charging his accusers with resisting the Holy Spirit and failing to live up to the true faith. The mob went wild with anger and accused him of blasphemy, when he claimed at that moment to have seen a vision of Paradise. Stephen was dragged outside the city and stoned to death. In the background of this terrible scene stood the young man Saul, watching over the garments of St. Stephen's executioners. Stephen was the first martyr of Christianity, the first witness of Christ.

Stephen's death marked the beginning of severe persecutions in Jerusalem, forcing the Christians to abandon that city and disperse to eastern Jordania, Judea, Samaria and Syria. This dispersion, as it was called, gave impulse to the missionary spirit in the early Church, so that by the end of the first century it had taken root in nearly all the lands bordering the Mediterranean and had gained a foothold in the Roman colonies of North Africa. A group of Greek Christians, it is thought, first colonized Gaul. By this time, Christianity had taken on a distinctly non-Jewish character. Its leaders stood ready to die for their Faith. The city of Jerusalem itself, with its beautiful temple built by Solomon, was destroyed by Titus in 70 A.D., as Christ had predicted would happen. The fierce nationalism of the Jews brought an end even to their colonial nationhood. Unmistakably, the church at Rome, which had been flourishing during the lifetime of St. Peter and St. Paul, had supplanted the church at Jerusalem as the center of Christianity.

Christ had warned his Apostles: "If they have persecuted me, they will persecute you also." The martyrs known to us by name, drawn from the writings of contemporaries and surviving records, number in the hundreds. The martyrs not known by name but who can be proved by their cult are counted in the thousands. One authority has assumed the total to be a number in six figures. Of the vast majority we know few details—only the manner of their death, their civic occupations, their age. Numerous are the legends about the martyrs, and this literature was much read during the Middle Ages and later centuries. When we add to the martyrs the number of confessors, who for the sake of their faith endured prison, torture, exile, confiscation and social ostracism, we begin to realize how valiant were the Christians in this Apostolic age, and how generously they served Christ. Moreover, their heroism influenced the religious life of countless Christians in later ages, even to this day. Above all else they demonstrated perfect constancy in serving God.

The Emperor Nero (54-68) is usually regarded as the originator of the persecutions, although there were martyrs, like St. Stephen, before his reign. No trace has ever been found of a formal law against Christians issued by Nero, so we must assume that the courts were instructed to deal with them as criminals. It proved convenient to blame the Christians for the burning of

Rome in 64 A.D., and so the persecutions raged from 64 to 68. A sounder legal basis for proceedings against Christians was provided when the Emperor Trajan (98-117) stated that they were to be punished if charges were made against them. The early Christians were persecuted because they refused to render to Caesar the things that are God's. According to Trajan's ruling, if an accused person declared his unwillingness to be a Christian any longer and proved this by paying homage to the Roman gods, or to the god-emperor, his guilty past would not be held against him. From this we can make the easy deduction that simply to be a Christian was to be a criminal. If the accused confessed that he was a Christian, his trial ended abruptly. The Roman judges were not bloodthirsty tyrants and generally tried every means, including coercion, to force the accused to carry out the required ceremonies so the death sentence could be avoided. In desperation, one Asian proconsul exclaimed: "You scoundrels, if you really want to die, jump off a cliff or go hang yourselves."

The educated Roman, as we know from passages in Latin literature, did not accept the proletariat's anti-Christian stories of cannibalism, child murder and so on. His complaint against Christians was not that they worshiped false gods but that they were atheists. They were persecuted because they rejected the polytheism of the state religion and opposed the recognition of the *numen* or divine character of the head of the state. In a phrase, they were bad citizens; their hostility to the established church was a form of treason. With intervals of relative peace, then, the infant Church was for over two and a half centuries a proscribed body, whose members met in secret for worship, instruction and the reception of the sacraments in those mazelike underground cemeteries we call the Catacombs. As the historian, Denis Meadows, tells us, "Christians revealing their religion by word or action were in danger of betrayal to the authorities, followed by arrest. Then would come the choice between apostasy and death, often a lingering one. Like all outlawed minorities, they evolved a technique for secrecy, including the sign of the fish, casually doodled with forefinger or sandaled toe, which served to identify a fellow believer. [The Greek word for fish was adopted because it was made up of the initial letters of the phrase, in Greek, 'Jesus Christ, Son of God, Savior.'] When the Church came out of the Catacombs, she was free to worship and to evangelize the pagans who . . . were stretching out their hands in unconscious love of the further shore. The martyrs had borne their witness; the story of their heroism aided the work of proselytism." [4]

II

Early Christian Apologists

In those first centuries of persecution and triumph, the martyrs were not the Faith's only defenders. Attacks on the Church by some of the most able pagan minds became more violent in the second century after St. John had completed his Gospels. Those who defended the Church against attack, and wrote on its behalf are called Christian "apologists." These Christian intellectuals felt they had an obligation to see if they could, by persuasion and teaching, move their pagan fellow men towards the study of the new religion. During the early Christian centuries a number of "the apologists" were martyrs as well as writers, thus leaving for posterity a twofold witness to the Faith.

Of these early apologists, St. Justin, or Justin Martyr (100-165), was a pagan turned confessor (*ca.* 130). After his conversion he wandered about the Near East, earning a living by his lectures. He was eager to reconcile all that was best in the thought of his day with Christian teaching. His *First Apology,* completed in 155, and his other writings reveal the central ideas behind mid-century attacks on Christians: their cult evoked pagan suspicions; they were charged with atheism for their refusal to worship the emperor; and they were accused of disloyalty to the state. Justin's writings openly admitted that the kingdom Christians

seek is not of this world. Along with six other Christians, he was tried before a Roman court, convicted
and beheaded in 165. As if in anticipation of the price
that refuting pagan writers would cost him, Justin
stated before the Roman Prefect that it was his desire
to suffer for the Lord Jesus Christ.

In the third century Christianity continued its spread
throughout North Africa, where it came to flourish
and find its most explicit definition until the Vandal
and Moslem onslaughts. From Carthage emerged the
effective voice of Tertullian (160-230), a lawyer converted around 195. In his *Apology* he exposed the
false accusations made against Christians. Instead of
being tortured until they confessed, he said, "Christians
are tortured until they deny." He observed that there
were never any witnesses to the awful crimes charged
against them. "Some say we are guilty of crimes. They
are uttering a new blasphemy against our God, for we
have not committed any. The future belongs to us."
He spoke of the martyr's blood as the Church's seed.
Tertullian later fell into heresy and founded a sect of
his own; nevertheless, his writings are one of our best
sources for an understanding of the relations between
the early Church and the Empire.

Like St. Justin, St. Irenaeus was bishop and martyr
(d. about 202). He came from Asia Minor, where he
listened, as a child, to the sermons of St. Polycarp,
Bishop of Smyrna. St. Irenaeus was later chosen Bishop
of Lyons in France, where he made many converts
among the pagans and lived up to his name, which is
Greek for "peacemaker." His best-known book, *Against
the Heresies*, was aimed at the Gnostics, a dissident
sect which emphasized that salvation is by knowledge.
the possession of the few. What brings St. Irenaeus

close to modern Catholic thinking is his insistence on the apostolic Roman See as the source and judge of what the Church teaches.[5] St. Irenaeus died as a martyr in the time of the Emperor Septimius Severus toward the end of the second century, according to the statement of St. Gregory of Tours.

Another apologist was St. Cyprian, Bishop of Carthage (249-258), who attempted to strengthen his office as a bulwark of Church organization. In a now-famous dispute with the Pope, St. Cyprian demanded that former heretics be permitted rebaptism, after reconciliation with the Church. Pope Stephen I (254-257) championed the Roman usage, later accepted by the entire Church, of recognizing heretical baptism as valid. Somewhat highhandedly the Pope attempted to impose his view on the Africans, but a council of African bishops supported Cyprian. Around this time, Cyprian produced a revised version of his *Treatise on Unity,* omitting affirmations of papal supremacy, and including implications that the Pope and his supporters were destroying church unity. Schism seemed imminent, but at that point Pope Stephen died and his successor, Sixtus II (257-58), allowed this matter of baptism to drop and left local churches free to follow their own practice. St. Cyprian died a victim of the Valerian persecution in 258. The courage, steadfast faith and spirit of the early Christians who faced the persecution of the state is contained in his famous utterance: "Let us stand up among the ruins and not lie on the ground with those who are without hope!"

An equally illustrious defense of the bishop's office appears in the second-century writings of Ignatius of Antioch. He merely assumed the lofty role of the bishop, and in elaborating on it, he was the first writer to use the term "Catholic Church": "Wherever the bishop appears, there let the people be, just as wheresoever Christ Jesus is, there is the Catholic Church."

From Alexandria in Egypt came Clement (150-215) and Origen (185-254), two noble defenders of the Faith. Overshadowing Clement was his more illustrious pupil, Origen, hailed as a universal genius for his breadth and depth of thought. He completed a six-column version of the Bible in that many languages, and he gave the world of theology the first authentic systematization of the Faith.

As great a company of theologians and thinkers as the Church has ever known gave their genius to these early centuries. Only a few of them are mentioned here. Others, like Hermas, Barnabas and Theophilus, deserve the attention space does not allow. Precursors of the age of ecumenical councils, they fought heresies in their separate traditions, entered the storm of persecution undaunted, suffered imprisonment and even death. Martyrs as well as writers, the early Christian apologists left for posterity a twofold witness to the Faith.

III

The Victory of Constantine

Some historians write of a series of ten persecutions beginning with that prompted by Nero in 64 A.D. and ending with the one under Diocletian in 305 A.D. In truth, ferment was constant during two centuries with only an occasional respite. Gradually the Faith began to attract men and women of all classes and stations. It survived the scourges of fanatical and insecure emperors, some of whom at times grew lax in their repression of Christianity. The conviction grew, in spite of persecution, that Christ's following could not be stamped out. Then came a revolutionary change: the persecuting Empire became tolerant of Christianity, embraced it as the official state religion and finally drew the sword to force its acceptance by all under Rome's sway.

The last systematic persecution of the Christians, and also the bitterest, under Diocletian ended with his abdicating the throne in 305 A.D. along with his co-ruler, Maximian. Once again anarchy threatened the Empire. The Caesars, or assistant emperors, now fought among themselves for supremacy. The momentous event in the struggle was the final victory of Constantine, one of the Caesars, over his last surviving rival in 312. Licinius and Maximinus had both claimed to be Augusti in the Eastern Empire. Constantine brought Licinius into an alliance with him, and then led their combined armies against Maxentius, in an effort to overthrow this tyrant who was ruler of northern Italy.

According to some versions of the story, on the eve of the battle, the pagan ruler, Constantine, had a dream or vision of an angel carrying the cross of Christ. The angel's voice told him: "In this sign thou shalt conquer." With hurried preparations, the initials in Greek for the name of Christ, (CHI RHO) were placed on the soldiers' helmets and the cross of Christ was inscribed on their standards. Giulio Romano's vivid painting in the Vatican recreates what followed. The city of Rome, fortified and protected by the Tiber River, presented a formidable obstacle to the invading army. Constantine attacked at the Milvian bridge where he was confronted by Maxentius and the defenders of Rome. The battle was close, but under the conquering sign Constantine's army had power beyond sword and spear. Though they were greatly outnumbered by the enemy, they succeeded in routing the cavalry of Maxentius and defeating his foot soldiers. Maxentius himself was drowned in the Tiber. Constantine is said to have exclaimed: "Oh, truly glorious providence of Christ our Lord!"

Some accounts of Constantine's vision were composed considerably after the event and critics have concluded that the story of the vision was later devised for propaganda purposes. There is, however, much evidence that the vision was a genuine experience of Constantine. Numerous Roman coins dating from 317 onward are inscribed with the Christogram. If the coins do not indicate an immediate adherence to Christianity following the victory, they at least show the trend away from paganism which historical accounts of the period have recorded.

After the victory at the Milvian bridge, two Augusti, Constantine in the West and Licinius in the East, now ruled the Empire together. The year after the battle they met at Milan in Italy and issued the famous edict which granted full religious toleration throughout all the territories of the Empire. This now put the Catholic religion on the same basis as polytheism, Judaism and Mithraism, along with various other Oriental sects. Eleven years later the two emperors quarrelled and Constantine defeated his former ally in battle. Licinius was spared at that time because his wife was half-sister to Constantine, but he was later put to death on a charge of conspiracy with the barbarian invaders.

Constantine was afterward revered as a saint by the Greek Orthodox Church. Elsewhere controversy still rages about the authenticity of his conversion, and the year it occurred. Strong evidence now points to the fact that, whatever his faith at the time of his great victory, he postponed baptism until he was dying, and then, Denis Meadows tells us, "it was given him by a priest who was a heretic and a sectary."[6]

No emperor before Constantine officially granted toleration to Christians. His granting it may have been chiefly a matter of political policy and expedience, but he soon went beyond that. He is noted for rebuilding ruined Christian churches, restoring property of the Church that had been seized, and tacitly recognizing the Church's special needs for an ordained ministry by abolishing the civic penalty for celibacy. Constantine also earns our respect for his humanitarianism when we are reminded that he did away with crucifixion as a form of punishment.

Whatever his motives and intentions, Constantine's policies improved the lot of Christians in all parts of the Empire but his concessions were not extended to the various groups of schismatic Christians. They extended only to those believers whose head was the Bishop of Rome, successor of St. Peter. The Edict of Milan was, therefore, no real triumph for the principle of toleration and the emperor's policy could prove, in time, a two-edged sword.

IV

.

The Church Fathers

The times called for learned men, steeped in theology, in the Sacred Scripture, trained in ancient and current philosophy, skilled with tongue and pen, capable of defining and teaching the doctrines of the new Faith. Happily the struggling Church had such a galaxy of writers and teachers in her early centuries. These men were true heirs of the Apostles in zeal and personal holiness.

The early Church Fathers are usually divided into two groups: the Greek Fathers of the Eastern Church and the Latin Fathers of the Western Church. In the former group we find St. Athanasius, St. Gregory Nazianzen, St. Basil and St. John Chrysostom. In the latter group are St. Jerome, St. Ambrose, St. Gregory the Great and St. Augustine. These men are distinguished by their sanctity, their ecclesiastical writings, and their sound teachings. Their genius was the glory of the young Church.

St. Athanasius (296-373) was born in Alexandria. He would have gained a distinguished reputation for his moral forcefulness and courage alone, but he was also a profound thinker and a great writer. At an early stage in his career he joined the fight for orthodoxy against the heresy known as Arianism. As a young deacon he accompanied his bishop to the Council of Nicaea (325) where his originality in finding new ways to express old truths was displayed. In 328 he was appointed to the See of Alexandria. Through almost a half-century as bishop, ending with his death in 373, his was the staunchest voice in the Eastern Empire, raised time after time in defense of orthodoxy and against Arianism, its hierarchy and government. His clear reasoning in defense of the true doctrine of the Incarnation made him Arianism's most powerful foe. On five occasions he was deposed and exiled. For one span of six or seven years, when his life was threatened, he disappeared altogether. We suspect he spent those years among his friends, the Egyptian desert monks, sharing in their enthusiasm for ascetic spirituality. On a visit to Rome, he brought to the West the first tidings of the foundation of the monasteries in Egypt. He is one of our few sources of knowledge about the early monastic movement, and his life of St. Anthony of Egypt is one of the earliest classics of religious biography. In fact, he is regarded as the creator of hagiography, the writing of histories of the saints. He was what St. Bernard called *vir ecclesiae,* "a man of the church," one of the outstanding churchmen of history.

The great Oriental theologian to whom we owe our correct belief in the Trinity and Incarnation was St. Basil (329-79), one of the most versatile and gifted of the Greek Fathers. Born in Caesarea, in Cappadocia, he studied at the schools of Constantinople and Athens, visited the monks of Palestine and Syria and then established a monastery. He was thus one of the chief organizers of ascetic community life in the East. At the great university of Athens, his fellow student and close friend was another young Cappadocian, St. Gregory Nazianzen, who, with the two brothers, Basil and Gregory of Nyssa, make up the trio of Cappadocian doctors of the Church.

In 370 St. Basil became Archbishop of his native Caesarea. At that time, the Arian heresy, which denied that Christ was God, or of the same substance with the Father, was at the high point of its influence. St. Basil became the well-balanced, driving spirit of the fight against Arianism, and the defense of the Catholic Faith against the Arian Emperor, Valens (364-78), who was vigorously persecuting the Catholics. St. Basil carried out his tasks with great courage, intellectual power, charity and a desire for agreement with his opponents unusual among theological controversialists. He so over-awed the Roman Prefect, and Emperor Valens that he and his diocese were left alone while persecutions raged all around them.

Besides defending the Catholic Faith against heresies, Basil wrote a theological work concerning the Holy Ghost, many discourses and letters, two important rules for monastic life, and he gave the example of being a model diocesan bishop. He visited every part of his diocese, organized a hospital for it, and preached frequent sermons. He lived to see the death of Valens and an end to the Arian persecutions, but he died very soon thereafter, at the age of forty-nine, worn out from many trials.

Possibly the greatest preacher among the Eastern Fathers was St. Gregory Nazianzen (329-90), who also studied at Athens with St. Basil and joined him for a time in a life of seclusion. In 379, after a period of troubled work at Nazianzus, where his father was bishop, and five more years of retreat, St. Gregory was invited to undertake the leadership of the orthodox Christians in Constantinople where the Arians were in control. There the popular method of solving religious controversies was by fighting in the streets or by a method even more distasteful to St. Gregory, intrigue. In spite of betrayals by his friends and annoyances from the Arian rabble, he stayed and delivered his famous sermons on the Trinity which won for him and for the Church increasing respect and renown. Even St. Jerome came in from the desert to hear him.

The Emperor Theodosius, nominated Emperor of the East in 379, declared against the Arians and recognized St. Gregory as Patriarch of the city (380-81). Gregory resigned this position in 381, however, because of a disagreement with the assembled bishops over an appointment to the patriarchate of Antioch. Returning to Nazianzus, this humble prelate served as bishop for a short time until another was chosen. Then he went into retirement, spending his last years in study, writing and mortification.

St. John Chrysostom (347-407) distinguished himself as an orator, moralist and interpreter of Sacred Scripture, particularly the epistles of St. Paul. His commentaries on them were so masterful that modern scholars have done little more than to elaborate on them. At thirty, St. John went to the Syrian desert to live as a hermit. Poor health forced him to return to his native Antioch, where he was assigned by his bishop to preach. His fame eventually reached Constantinople, to which the Eastern Emperor invited him to come as patriarch. St. John, as Archbishop of that great city, directed his efforts toward cutting down diocesan expenses, giving money to the poor (his own income was largely spent on hospitals, and other good works in his See), founding convents, reforming the clergy, elevating the moral standards of Christians, and even fearlessly denouncing the laxity of the Empress Eudoxia (whom he called "Jezebel") and her courtiers. A cabal finally persuaded the Empress to banish St. John, and while the old man was being hurried on the journey from one place of exile to another, his strength gave out. He was taken to the chapel of St. Basilicus near Comana in Cappadocia, where he died. After the saint's death, Pope Innocent I compelled the submission of his enemies (which included the spiteful Empress Eudoxia and Archbishop Theophilus of Alexandria), and in 438 the body of St. John was brought back in solemn procession to Constantinople, the new Emperor and his sister doing penance for the sins of their parents.

Four other great saints were the pillars of medieval culture, each making his contribution in a particular field of knowledge. Through St. Ambrose (339-397), much of Origen's earlier learning and genius were brought to the Western Church. Ambrose was born in what is now Trier, of a family of distinguished Roman officials. His father was prefect of the Gauls. Ambrose was sent to Rome for a legal education and on its completion he was appointed governor of Liguria. While attending a meeting to elect the new Bishop of Milan, Ambrose was spontaneously chosen for the office even though he had not yet been baptized a Christian. After baptism and holy orders, he entered upon a life of distinguished Church service. As Bishop of Milan, Ambrose demonstrated his ability as an administrator in the great tradition of Roman government and as a forceful writer and speaker.

His career was marked by several sharp clashes with the Emperor, for Ambrose set down a theological position for the Christian ruler within the Church and a statement on the Church's moral authority restricting the power of autocratic rulers in their public acts. "The emperor is within the Church, not over the Church," he wrote. Thus, when Theodosius was guilty of the brutal massacre of some five thousand rebels in an insurrection at Thessalonica, Ambrose denied him the sacraments and excommunicated him. Theodosius resisted for a while but finally did public penance and was reinstated in the Church by Bishop Ambrose.

Unlike some of the other Church Fathers, St. Ambrose's vocation was pastoral, not literary. He introduced the Eastern custom of singing hymns into the Western Church, and wrote several hymns himself (*"Veni Redemptor Omnium"*), along with several elaborate treatises on virginity and faith. It is as devoted pastor to his flock that he is seen by his greatest convert, St. Augustine, who was baptized at his hand in 387.

A contemporary of St. Ambrose was St. Jerome (342-420). Born at Stridon in Dalmatia of well-to-do Christian parents, Jerome received a good literary and rhetorical education first at Stridon, then under the famous grammarian, Donatus at Rome. He joined an informal community of ascetics in 370 and he later went east to live as a hermit in the desert of Chalcis, where he had no company "but scorpions and wild beasts," and where he suffered greatly from ill health and temptation. There he began the study of Hebrew, thus embarking on his real life work as a scholar devoted to the work of translating and interpreting the Scriptures.

At the suggestion of Pope Damasus I (366-84), St. Jerome undertook to make a reliable Latin translation of the Gospels and the Psalms. The name "Vulgate" was later applied to St. Jerome's Latin translation of the Bible from the Greek which was declared the accepted version for Catholics by the Council of Trent. For this great work, and for his commentaries on the Old Testament, he has been given the title, "Doctor of Sacred Scripture."

St. Jerome also vigorously encouraged the movement toward the ascetic life which was then developing among some of the great ladies of Rome. He attacked worldliness in picturesque but intemperate language, in consequence of which he became extremely unpopular, and after the death of St. Damasus in 384 Jerome withdrew into seclusion in the East. A group of Roman ladies living the religious life under his direction followed him. They included St. Paula and her daughter, St. Eustochium, and together they founded a group of convents near the cave of St. Jerome. The cell, in which he lived with a lion for protection, is still to be seen at the Basilica of the Nativity in Bethlehem. Here Jerome spent the remaining years of his life until he died at the age of eighty-one. He built monasteries for men and women, served as abbot and pastor, and continued his Biblical studies. In the years between 385 and 405 he completed the revision of the Bible and it is on this that his authority in the Catholic Church rests.

St. Augustine of Hippo (354-430) is one of those key figures who belongs to all ages. He represents the culmination of theological genius and literary mastery in the early Church. Two of the greatest books of all times were his work: *The City of God,* which he wrote during the barbarian invasions of Rome and in which he showed that Christianity was not responsible for Alaric's successful attack in 410, and *The Confessions,* an autobiography in which he traces the steps from his dissolute youth through religious trials and experiences to a triumphant conversion and dedication to the service of the vigorous young Church in North Africa.

Born in Tagaste, in African Numidia, Augustine was educated in the best classical tradition and his saintly mother, Monica, saw to it that he was given Christian teaching. He became a professor of rhetoric at Car-

thage, at Rome, and eventually at Milan, which was
then the capital of the Western empire. Here he first
heard the sermons of St. Ambrose, whose influence
finally brought about his conversion. After years of
contemplation, study and writing, he was called in 396
to the bishop's See at Hippo where he remained until
his death in 430. He showed great zeal in caring for
the souls in his flock, combating the heresies of Do-
natism and Pelagianism and adding to the monumental
literary production that was the marvel of the medieval
world. Augustine linked the old era with the new.
Many medieval historians begin their record with him.
More than any other of the Church Fathers he made
Latin culture part of the Catholic tradition which passed
into the Middle Ages to become the heritage of subsequent times.

Like St. Augustine, Pope St. Gregory the Great (540-
604) was a link between the age of barbarism and the
medieval age of missionary activity which saw the conversion of Northern Europe. Gregory became a Benedictine monk, after pursuing a legal and political career
for some years. He converted his home in Rome into
a monastery and served for a time as papal representative to Constantinople. In 590 he was called from his
monastery where he was then abbot to the chair of
St. Peter, which he ascended with great reluctance.

St. Gregory the Great made the medieval Papacy a
real power in Western Europe and molded it in its
relations with the West. He was a careful husbandman
of the Church's patrimony, wisely administering its
lands in northern Italy and Sicily. He dispensed the
Church's wealth for the care of Rome's poor. To the
development of plainsong, or Gregorian chant, as it
is now known, he made an obscure but certain contribution. A popular work was his handbook of in-

structions for bishops called *Pastoral Care*. His pontificate lasted fourteen years—during which the Roman Empire was falling apart. He asserted the principle of the primacy of Peter unswervingly; he reorganized the Church, amalgamating dioceses; he reformed the papal household; he instituted the devotion, "the Stations of the Cross"; and he is known as the Apostle of England for having dispatched St. Augustine and his monks to convert the pagan Saxons. Many other liturgical reforms are attributed to St. Gregory. Aptly has he been called "the Servant of the Servants of God." His first tomb bore a Latin inscription which sums up the great Pope's life in a single phrase: he is here called "God's Consul." The consuls of republican Rome had gone; imperial Rome herself was already experiencing her death agonies. But St. Gregory stands as a link between the age of the patricians and that of the pontiffs, between the glory that was the historical city of Rome and the glory of the City of God.

V

Early Monasteries

There were those in early Christian times who sought the higher counsels of perfection in what came to be called the monastic life. Monasticism was a movement which got under way in the middle of the third century and it has had an unbroken history from that time to the present. The name "monasticism" comes from a Greek adjective meaning "alone." At first it was a matter of individual religious life for men and women who later withdrew from society to devote themselves in seclusion to the worship of God and devotion to the spiritual life. Early ascetics, lacking the opportunities modern organized religious orders afford, stayed within their family circle and practiced a rigid routine of prayer, fasting and charitable works. Many also took a vow of chastity. Others withdrew into desert regions where they constructed rude mud and wattle huts, or occupied empty tombs, abandoned forts or natural caves, often sharing these dwellings with the local fauna. They spent long hours in prayer, meditation, fasting and manual labor. These people were called hermits or anchorites.

The traditional founder of Christian monasticism (we find similar practices in some non-Christian sects) was St. Paul of Thebes, about whom we know very little except that he was a holy recluse who lived a long life at the end of which was formed the friendship with St. Anthony of Egypt.

St. Anthony is credited with having encouraged monasticism as a definite way of life. He was born in the valley of the Nile about sixty miles below Cairo, where he received only the rudiments of an education. He inherited, with a sister, the family property, which he sold or gave away and then retired to the desert, first in Egypt, then in Syria, and for a time in Arabia. He sought only solitude and silence for himself but involuntarily he seems to have sparked a movement, for others came, built hermitages in the desert near his and came to look upon him as their beloved master. He could hardly avoid being father and guide to these spiritual aspirants.

Egypt seems to have been the location selected as the cradle of monastic life because of its geographic features. As the severity of persecutions increased, more Christians fled to its isolation in order to escape. St. Anthony spent twenty years in the solitude of an abandoned fort on the banks of the Nile. Soon more than a thousand hermits populated the hills and deserts of Nitria, Cellia and Scete. In 305 Anthony left his lonely outpost long enough to organize a community of "hermits." There was little of common life but for the first time men lived near each other on an organized basis under an established rule. Some who came to the Egyptian desert merely to escape persecution became so inured to the monastic life that they decided to remain. A number of hermits visited St. Anthony and were so impressed by his holiness and wisdom that they settled near him. One of these visitors was St. Paul of Thebes. Soon St. Anthony was recognized as the leader of the anchorites in the desert region of northern Egypt. He spent the latter part of his life in solitude building his hermitage by the Red Sea on a mountain that still bears his name today.

St. Pachomius developed the work begun by St. Anthony. The task of consolidating and organizing monasticism fell largely to him. He drew up the first monastic rule, formulating the principles of asceticism and established a large monastery at Tabennisi, which lies to the north of Luxor, sometime before the middle of the fourth century. Here on the banks of the Nile the monks shared common buildings surrounded by high walls. All followed the same rule and wore uniform dress. Self-sufficient groups, known as Cenobites, from the Greek word meaning "common life," were housed in different buildings according to their skills. Manual labor was essential to this system, in which rules of holy living for men and also women were emphasized. Through the centuries the most far-reaching patterns established by Pachomius were this life in common and the full authority granted to abbots.

Egypt, however, was not the sole center of eremitical life. Many holy souls followed St. Jerome to Palestine, where they practiced asceticism. In Syria, recluses had themselves walled into cells. Some, like St. Simeon Stylites, lived on platforms atop pillars where they preached the Gospel and interceded for the sins of men.

In time, numbers of monks followed the Pachomian ideal in Italy, Spain, France and Africa. St. Martin of Tours (316-397) followed his vocation as a solitary and established a monastery at Marmoutier (near Poitiers) on the Loire in the latter part of the fourth century. This was probably the first monastic settlement in the Western world. The main significance of St. Martin's monks was their devotion to Christianizing the country people of Europe. St. Martin was elected Bishop of Tours in 372 and became a religious leader in Gaul.

The Church honors him today as confessor. Around his tomb pilgrims gather and miracles have been reported wrought by his intercession. Innumerable churches throughout Europe have been dedicated to St. Martin of Tours, four thousand of them in France alone, and five hundred French villages bear his name.

To the Near East St. Basil brought the ideals of monastic life learned on a tour of Syrian and Egyptian laurae (the Greek name for monasteries where the monks lived). Other ascetics joined him after 350 and together they founded a monastery near Neocaesarea, for which Basil supplied a core of principles of monastic living, emphasizing his preference for the communal over solitary existence. He said: "If you always live alone, whose feet will you wash?" Under his rule, meals, work and worship were all shared in common within the same house. A novitiate was provided for the training of young aspirants and the number of monks in each house was kept small. The rule emphasized charitable service to others; thus he introduced the work of monks in hospitals, teaching and providing for travelers.

Early in the sixth century the West received a basic plan for its monastic system, a truly great rule from the hands of St. Benedict of Nursia. About forty miles southeast of Rome the Emperor Nero had once built a summer home for himself. To this same spot, in a cave called Subiaco, Benedict retreated to live as a hermit. His exemplary devotion attracted many followers, for whom he founded nearby monasteries. Local jealousies and intrigue forced him to leave with a band of followers for southern Italy. Halfway to Naples, in 529, they climbed a mountain (Monte Cassino), and on this ideal site they decided to rear a monastery. They converted the local country people and laid the foundations of one of the greatest monastic centers in the Western world. Monte Cassino was the nursery for saints and scholars for more than fifteen centuries.[7] The monastery's most famous pupil was destined to be St. Thomas Aquinas. It became the mother house for the Benedictine order and St. Benedict's rule became the guide for more than 25,000 religious who bear his name. The monastery was destined to be destroyed over and over again, the last time by Allied bombers and artillery fire in World War II. But once again the monks began patiently to rebuild and to revive the spirit that once permeated those ancient walls.

The pattern of St. Benedict's system provided a new ideal of service in holiness to God. Noted for its moderation, his rule called for obedience, silence, humility, poverty, chastity and the recitation of the Divine Office. Monks were allowed moderate amounts of food (no meat) and wine and an average of eight hours sleep. Prayers and manual labor were the chief duties within monastery walls where everything necessary for daily life was situated. Pope St. Gregory the Great, who first sent St. Augustine and twelve Benedictine monks to establish a mission in England in 596, was responsible for influencing many of the Benedictines to become missionary priests.

Soon the chain of monasteries described a great arc around the Mediterranean and into Western Europe. The monks preserved learning and culture during the invasions of barbarians, and through the ages set ideals of holiness and piety. The Benedictines, in particular, have held a leading place during all this time as exemplars and propagators of liturgical worship according to the Roman rite.[8]

VI

Byzantium

After Constantine established himself as the sole ruler of the Roman Empire, he established a new capital. Rome was no longer the real center of the Empire— ill-situated as it was far from the northern and eastern frontiers. He finally chose the site for his new Rome; in 324 A.D. he strode around the jutting promontory on the shores of the Black Sea and with a spear marked out the fortifications for the new city—once called Byzantium in ancient Greece. It was renamed Constantinople. Ideally situated as a military and administrative headquarters at the junction of East and West, the city took five and a half years to complete. Constantine desired to establish a Christian capital distinct from Rome and uncontaminated by pagan reaction. Pagan sacrifice, essential to its worship, was banished from Constantine's city. He filled its magnificent buildings with rich furnishings and decorations—the plunder of the empire. Here a contemplative life developed, monasteries and convents were founded, magnificent art, music and architecture flourished—a whole new civilization emerged. This Byzantine Empire, as it was later known, colored with semi-Oriental splendor and dominated by a long dynasty of Christian priest-kings, was to flourish for over a thousand years, and was the bulwark of the Western world against both barbarians and Moslems. It was the first Christian state, the breeding ground of some of the Church's worst heresies, and much of its highest spirituality.

In the East great heresies arose which troubled the Church in the fourth and fifth centuries. One of the most dangerous of them involved the teaching of the Alexandrian priest, Arius. Arianism held that since Christ was begotten of the Father and did not exist from eternity, He is not God. This heresy did more harm to the Church than any other doctrinal dispute until the Protestant revolt. A synod at Alexandria in 318, attended by 100 bishops, condemned the heresy but the Arians refused to submit to its authority. Finally, in 325 Constantine, though not yet a Christian, called the Council of Nicaea, where a definition of faith similar to the Apostle's Creed was introduced and defended by St. Athanasius with the insertion of words proclaiming the Son of God "true God of true God . . . begotten not made . . . consubstantial with the Father." Arianism was condemned and Arius excommunicated.

The first ecumenical council set a pattern for later councils and was of great historical importance. However, Arianism remained strong and its adherents were powerful enough to bring about the banishment of St. Athanasius. The intervention of Constantine demonstrates the growing influence of Eastern emperors over religious matters. The first eight ecumenical councils were called by Byzantine emperors who often treated the Pope like a court official. Violent conflicts arose between the Eastern episcopate and the Roman Pontiffs. In the fifth century came the first schism. The Eastern Church used as the official tongue the Greek language rather than the Latin, and thereafter tended to become an independent institution, while remaining closely bound to the state that ruled it. Complex arguments over doctrinal disputes and theological arguments kept the Eastern Church in constant turmoil. The efforts of the emperors to dominate the Church resulted in what is called "Caesaropapism" and it prevailed mainly in the East.

In 402 A.D., when fleeing from barbarian invaders, the emperor of the Western Roman Empire sought refuge in Ravenna, a well-protected inland city yet accessible by sea to Constantinople (via the port of Classe). While battles raged without, within Ravenna's walls a series of majestic churches were erected, embellished in the ancient art of mosaics, with gold and precious stones. As the strict and ruthless upholder of the Orthodox faith, the Emperor Justinian (527-565) dominated Ravenna and the Mediterranean world for more than a quarter of a century. Under him, Byzantium attained its peak of power and achievement. The last of the Latin-speaking rulers, he dreamed of restoring Christian and Roman unity, for he alone, of all the many rulers of Byzantium, shared Constantine's view of Church and state. From the beginning of his reign until his death in 565 A.D. he sent his armies to conquer Italy, Spain, Africa and Asia Minor. Thus Italy was united to the Byzantine Empire and ruled by Justinian's representative, called the exarch, who resided at Ravenna. Even the Frankish kings of Gaul recognized Justinian's suzerainty. His attempt to restore the splendors of imperial Rome was impractical and largely a failure, but D. M. Nicol wrote: "It was a glorious failure."

The range of Justinian's activities was extraordinary. His generals won back North Africa from the Vandals and destroyed the Ostrogothic kingdom in Italy. Two lasting monuments stand as testimony to the genius of Justinian: the law code which bears his name and the great cathedral, Hagia Sophia. After gaining the throne in 527 in a high-handed *coup d'état,* he ordered a full revision of the old Roman law; the resulting code is the basis for much Western law and for canon law. In seeking to surround the seat of majesty with fitting splendor, he sponsored magnificent architectural masterpieces; hence the luxury of the Sacred Palace. It was said that the new Rome contained as many churches as there are days in the year. Hagia Sophia (or St. Sophia), the Church of the Holy Wisdom, was completed by Justinian in Byzantium's golden age and stands today as an enduring symbol of his ideal. This church exemplifies many of his architectural innovations. The lofty dome, 184 feet high and 102 feet in diameter, demanded previously untried engineering concepts so his engineers developed a new cement to withstand the tremendous stress placed upon half-domes, walls and arches. To viewers, the dome seemed to float incredibly over an enormous empty space "as if suspended from the heavens by a golden chain." After its completion by ten thousand workmen in five years, at a cost of 320,000 pounds of gold, it is said when Justinian first entered its doors, he exclaimed: "Glory to God who hath deemed me worthy of so great a work. I have outdone thee, Solomon."

As a champion of orthodoxy and the propagation of the faith, Justinian formed a close alliance with the Papacy. But it was also his aim to unite Church and state under his single control. Thus in the reign of Justinian Cæsaropapism gained ground within the Eastern Empire. The Emperor, he thought (the actual term for emperor was "Basileus"), and not the Pope, should make all major decisions. Absolute rulers from ancient times to modern totalitarian regimes have always reacted in identical fashion toward the Church. In his later years Justinian veered more and more toward heresy and even tried to force the Pope to subscribe to his heretical views. After his death in 565, the Eastern Empire and the Church, held together precariously by his strong will, were again the prey of hostile forces.

In the eighth century a Frankish ruler named Pepin consolidated the Western kingdoms under a new dynasty allied to the Holy See. In Italy, Pepin defeated the Lombards and awarded Ravenna and part of Umbria to the Pope. In 800 his son, Charlemagne, was crowned by Pope Leo III successor in the West to the old Roman emperors. Charlemagne proceeded to unify most of Europe, and thus came into being the Holy Roman Empire, a centralized political unity based on St. Augustine's concept of a Christian community set forth in his *City of God*. Thus, after 800, Eastern emperors no longer exercised any political or religious influence in the West. This was another factor in straining relations between the churches of Constantinople and Rome. From then on Byzantium stood alone, and though her fortunes were to rise and fall many times, the trend was toward slow but steady decline.

VII

Mohammed and Islam

While the barbarian tribes that swept across the Rhine and Danube were being absorbed into the Christian body, while young nations laid the foundations of Christian Europe, while the Pope came to replace the emperor as Pontifex Maximus, and while missionaries labored to advance the Faith among the people of Northern Europe, a new source of opposition to Christianity was taking form in Arabia. In the pontificate of Gregory the Great, the camel driver, Mohammed (570-632), began formulating his religious concepts. His religion, which was destined to revolutionize the East, is called Islam, because its followers believed in predestination, or complete resignation to the decrees of God. The common name Mohammedanism given to this religion is misleading because Moslems do not regard Mohammed as its founder but trace its origins back through the prophets (Abraham, Moses, etc.) to God's revelation to Adam. Jesus Christ himself was incorporated in the teachings of Mohammed. For Moslems, however, He is no longer the Son of God but only another prophet. Islam is a simple creed, borrowing elements from Judaism and the Monophysite heresy of Arabian Christians. It teaches that there is one God, Allah, that Mohammed is his greatest prophet, and God's revelations to him and God's final word are incorporated in the Sacred book called the Koran, completed after Mohammed's death. The followers of Islam are called Moslems, signifying surrender to God. On every Moslem believer rested the sacred obligation to propagate his faith, destroy the unbeliever and wage a holy war for Moslem goals.

Between 636 and 641 Syria, Palestine and Egypt fell into Moslem hands, the Arabian peninsula was overrun and the Persian empire was vanquished by these hard-riding men of the desert. Thus the very lands that had witnessed the great events of primitive Christianity, and that had produced the Church's scholars and martyrs, were now lost, and Christianity in these regions was destined to wither away. The flood of Moslem victories swept all before it. Fifty years after Mohammed's death, the Moors, as Moslems were known in the West, invaded Roman Africa; in 711 they crossed into Spain via Gibraltar and then overran southern Gaul. In 717 they laid siege to Constantinople, which was only saved by the military skill of the Byzantine Emperor, Leo III. Six times in six years the Moslems assaulted that Eastern stronghold and each time they failed. While the Church in the East was convulsed with unnecessary theological disputes, Charles Martel, ruler of the Gauls, repelled the western advance of the Moors in the bloody battle of Tours (732) near Poitiers, where he gained the name "the Hammer." Had he not halted the Moslem advance, all Europe might have come under the sway of Islam. Even so, the entire Mediterranean was now a Moslem lake, and for another nine hundred years Christendom would be assaulted in every generation from some quarter of the Moslem world.

At the outset, Mohammed and some of his followers treated Christians leniently but after some time this attitude changed. Submission, tribute and surrender were rewarded with some indulgence, even toward those who did not embrace Islam, but resistance meant war to the death.

Omar, Mohammed's cousin, succeeded him as caliph in 634 and was responsible for the important capture of Jerusalem in 637 and Alexandria in 639. A succession of later rulers made a dynasty of the Caliphate and moved the capital to Baghdad, where the empire's leaders became so preoccupied with court life that rule passed into the hands of their own slaves and mercenaries—the Seljuk Turks. This fierce breed of militant Moslems fought the Crusades to an inconclusive standstill, only to be temporarily overrun by the Mongol armies of Genghis Khan. So it was left to a small band of fugitives from the Mongol hordes—the Ottoman Turks—to take up the Islamic banner. At one point it seemed as if the Turks, whose sultans were caliphs of the modern world for five centuries, might conquer all of Europe, for under Suleiman the Magnificent, they stormed the very gates of Vienna. A combined army of European states halted the spread of Islam to the West but in the East, Mohammed II, the Ottoman sultan, and his armies finally laid successful siege to and captured Constantinople in 1453, thus putting an end to the Eastern Roman Empire. The great edifice Hagia Sophia was transformed into a Moslem mosque. In Sicily, Spain and elsewhere in Southern Europe, many a church standing today is a transformed mosque, attesting to the wealth and luxury of Mohammed's successors and also to the high civilization and culture they brought to Europe. The Spanish-Arab philosopher Averroës, for example, wrote a book of commentaries on Aristotle which served European scholarship for a long time; even St. Thomas Aquinas was a respectful student of the Arab philosopher.

There are almost three hundred million Moslems today. No other people are more impervious to the teaching of Christianity, for converts to other faiths are ousted from Islamic society and even persecuted.

VIII

The Conversion of Western Europe

After the conversion of the Emperor Constantine to Christianity in the fourth century, the entire Roman world eventually came to embrace the new Faith. The doctrine of Jesus and the Apostles was destined at last to spread beyond the confines of the Empire to distant lands and people. The fresh spirit embodied in the teachings of the Christian Church, which for long had been obliged to exist in secret and under repression, was now set free to make its rapid way. A new force was infused into the Empire which helped to maintain it for another century and a half, and which ultimately transmitted through the "Dark Ages" some tradition and recollection of a political ideal superior to that of the petty state.

To the north of the Roman world lived tribes of Germans or Teutons, called barbarians (though they were not savages). These were the Goths, Vandals, Franks, Lombards, Saxons, Angles and Jutes. On the steppes of Central Asia lived another tribe called the Huns, noted for the cruelty and destructiveness of their invasions. Their religion was a mixture of polytheism, ancestor worship and reverence for nature. Rome had experienced difficulty earlier with these northern tribes, which were attracted by Roman riches, driven to seek grazing and pasture lands, and encouraged in their expansion by the steady decay of Roman institutions. In 410, Alaric, the leader of the Visigoths, captured

Rome and sacked the city. Later, the Vandals overran it and pushed on to imperial outposts in North Africa. Then came the Huns, led by Attila, their king, called "the scourge of God."

It was later discovered that the Eastern Emperor at Constantinople had made secret treaties with the barbarian invaders, to the effect that if they spared the Eastern portion of the Empire, their incursions into Italy would not be interfered with by imperial troops. In the meantime, the people of central Italy threw themselves into the arms of the Pontiff for the protection they could no longer expect from any other source. The Pope left nothing undone to correspond with their wishes; in famine, in pestilence, amid the desolations of carnage, the Popes were, if not the protectors of the people, at least their fathers and comforters. In his solicitude for his flock, the chief Pastor at Rome even risked his life to defend them.

In 452, the Huns, led by Attila, poured into northern Italy and, after leaving desolation in their path, marched on Rome. As terror struck the citizens and even the Emperor and General looked to him, Pope Leo I (440-61) went out with his clergy from the city and held open parley with Attila, who consented to spare the city on the payment of an annual tribute. Tradition has it that as Leo spoke to the devastating commander, Attila saw in the air over the Pope's head the figures of the Apostles, Peter and Paul with drawn swords, threatening instant destruction of himself and his army should it attempt to enter the Holy City.

Three years later, Genseric, the leader of the Vandals, was less amenable to the great Pope but even then Leo's influence was strong enough to make the Vandals stop short of looting the city, setting fire to it and murdering the people. Like Pope Leo, subsequent Popes continued to assist the people of Italy, employing papal incomes in rebuilding Rome's defenses, churches and homes. They sent into plundered districts whole fleets laden with grain and lent their aid when no other aid or encouragement could be found.

These barbarian invasions of the Roman Empire represented both a great threat to the Faith and later, a great opportunity. When they were over, Rome disappeared as a power in the political world. The Eastern Empire alone carried on the Roman traditions with its capital at Constantinople. Critical historians are partially correct in concluding that, by its displacement of the religion of imperial loyalty, its accent on asceticism and its de-emphasis on military ideals, Christianity had something to do with the collapse of the Roman government. However, Christianity was only one factor in the decline. No emperor of importance had lived in Rome for the last hundred and forty years and the city no longer enjoyed the importance politically that it had at the time of Augustus or even of Marcus Aurelius.

Even before the invasions the Christian Faith had penetrated the pagan tribes in the north. St. Justin spoke of Christianity among the barbarians as early as 165. In the fourth century, the Council for the Church in the West was held at Arles in Gaul (314) and was attended by the bishops of Cologne and Metz.

From 481 to 511 the Emperor of the Franks was Clovis, whose wife was the Christian Clotilda, later canonized a saint. In a battle experience which resembles that of Constantine, Clovis prayed to the God of Clotilda. After the victory Clovis was baptized a Christian by St. Remigius, Bishop of Rheims. Within the year, three thousand of his subjects followed his example. Thus Christianity came to Gaul, which in the sixth and seventh centuries was slowly turning into France. The Franks went on to conquer most of Gaul, which became one of the great Christian centers of the world through the efforts of monks from southern Gaul, Italy and Ireland. Alone among the barbarian tribes, the Franks survived to become a powerful nation in Europe.

It was St. Patrick (392-461), the first great monk-missioner, who not only founded monasteries but converted Ireland to Catholicism. Thus he was instrumental in making the land where he had been held a slave for six years that great center of culture and monasteries from which missionaries would one day set forth to enlighten Europe. Patrick was trained in Gaul, ministered for a time in the church at Auxerre, and was consecrated bishop to undertake the mission to Ireland, unsuccessfully attempted by Palladius. The most cynical historian is forced to marvel at the unbelievable effectiveness of Patrick's preaching and the conversions which followed in the last thirty years of his life.

We know that the Catholic Faith had reached the British Isles before 300 for the bishops of London, Lincoln and York attended the Council of Arles in 314. The Roman outposts established there by Julius Caesar as early as 55 B.C. were not spared destruction by the barbarians, who so savagely hated the Christians that the English bishops refused to attempt their conversion.

One of the greatest achievements of Pope St. Gregory the Great (590-604) was his decision to send a mission to convert the English. Under the leadership of another Augustine, this band of Benedictine monks landed in Kent in 597 and almost immediately Augustine was on good terms with King Ethelbert. His wife,

Bertha, was already a Christian for she was grand-daughter to the Frankish king, Clovis. Under her influence, Ethelbert was willing to accept the Christian teachings of Augustine and his monks. Many of his subjects followed King Ethelbert into the Church. It was in southeastern England that St. Augustine established what was to become the center of English Christianity—the See of Canterbury. Fittingly, this great missionary who had done so much to plant the Faith vigorously in England before his death in 605 was its first bishop and was later canonized.

Before long, zealous Irish monks from the island monastery of Iona, founded by the elder Columba in 563, were achieving similar triumphs in the north. They landed in Scotland and England before turning westward to the continent. St. Columba (521-597) led a small band of monks to Scotland in 563. From Iona he governed the numerous monasteries established by him to aid in the conversion of Scotland and Wales. The fame of the Irish monks spread far and wide. King Oswald of Northumbria asked for monks from Iona, who soon established themselves in another monastery on another island—Lindisfarne, in 634. Together these monks made northern England a Catholic stronghold. The first centers of culture were the monasteries. Here the monks taught the native priests and bishops the Latin tongue, thus establishing the roots of that association between Catholicism and literary culture which for centuries marked the Irish Church. When the Latin language had all but perished elsewhere, even in Italy, knowledge of it survived in this one Western land where the Romans had never set foot, and this knowledge, carried back to Europe by Irish monk missionaries, supplied the beginnings of the later European renaissance.[9]

From the monastery of Bangor near Belfast, St. Columbanus (550-615) led a dozen monks in 590 to Brittany in Europe, where they preached penance and reform in an effort to restore the holiness of Christian life to the people of Gaul and the decadent court of the Frankish kings. They were invited by the King of Burgundy to found a number of monasteries in his kingdom. From there they expanded their mission to Alsace, Switzerland and northern Italy. All along their route monasteries sprang up—Annegray, Fontaines and Luxeuil, where St. Columbanus composed his monastic rule. After preaching in the region around Lake Constance, St. Columbanus and his followers went to the Lombard kingdom in Upper Italy, where they were warmly received by King Agilulf and his Christian wife, Theodelinda. They encouraged the monks to remain among them and endowed them with a grant of land between Genoa and Milan. Here, in 612, was established the greatest monastery of them all, Bobbio, which became famous as a stronghold of Catholicism against Arianism. There, in 615, St. Columbanus died. He had left Gallus, his friend and companion for many years, behind at Lake Constance on the Swiss side where he lived as a hermit. Soon, however, other monks gathered there and the hermitage of St. Gall became the nucleus of the monastery of St. Gall, which was richly endowed by Charles Martel and Pepin the Short. On the island of Reichenau in Lake Constance, St. Pirnan later founded another monastery, which had a famous scriptorium in Ottonian times. The church at the eastern tip of the island is said to be the oldest in Germany.

St. Columbanus and his followers, who preached the Gospel for the first time in Belgium, Luxemburg, Lorraine and Bavaria, were the forerunners of the most important of all religious orders, that of St. Benedict. Scarcely anything survives today of buildings from the time of Columbanus. The monasteries founded by him and his followers all eventually accepted the Benedictine rule, for the rule which Columbanus gave to his monks was brief and harsh. This rule was the expression of the Irish nationality, whose culture in the period from 650 to 750 derived entirely from monasticism. In asceticism the Irish monks rivaled the austerity of the Egyptians. A popular saying described their life as "the white martyrdom." Food was scant and never included meat; fasts were long; sleep was limited and disrupted by many prayers. The Celtic monks often prayed with arms extended in the form of a cross. They erected fine buildings, many of whose upward-tapering cylindrical towers still stand as landmarks in Ireland, as for example, the one at Lendalough. The ancient Irish stone crosses, dedicated to different saints, are still to be found in England, Scotland and the Isle of Man, testifying to the early missionary activity of the Irish monks.

They achieved a high perfection in church articles, such as the famed Ardagh chalice and the reliquary of St. Patrick's bell. The ninth-century *Book of Kells* has a series of magnificent illuminations, including an initial page which shows their extraordinary, painstaking craftsmanship. Their forms of artistry were raised to the highest and most sophisticated level of which medieval art was capable.

The strict discipline of St. Columbanus was enforced for some time in the monasteries of Gaul and the Rhineland until the arrival of Benedictines from across the Alps. The Benedictines were as pious as the Irish monks and as active in charitable works, but their rule was milder. Othmar, said to have been the first abbot of St. Gall, introduced the Benedictine monastic rule and founded the School of St. Gall, which became a stronghold of learning in Europe. During the Middle Ages it became a leading European center of literature and the arts, particularly music. Its famous library in large part still survives, adjoining the cathedral dedicated to St. Gall. North of the Alps, St. Gall became the principal monastery of the Benedictines of Monte Cassino.

Two missionaries carried the Gospel to the Low Countries and northern Germany: Willibrord and Boniface. Willibrord (658-739) had been trained by the Irish monks. From his episcopal See at Utrecht he set forth to preach in Frisia and Denmark. At Echternach he founded a famous monastery from which later missions emerged. Among the monks he trained was one Winfrith, later named by Pope Gregory II Boniface ("he who does good"). St. Boniface (675-754) is often called the Apostle of Germany. No other European accomplished so much for the Church in Europe. Not only did he convert a large part of central Germany but he also reformed the Church in Gaul and gave to German Catholicism its organization. His policy was based on the realization that the only way to secure Christianity's hold on the new territories was by means of a firm organization, which he knew Rome alone could not supply. What was also needed was the support of the temporal power in these newly converted lands.

For thirty years Boniface labored in Hesse, Thuringia and Saxony, where he was careful to make no violent attacks on pagan beliefs, merely pointing out errors and contradictions. In the last years of his life he returned to Frisia to fulfill an earlier dream—that of evangelizing the savage pagans there. In 754 a martyr's death crowned a long life of service for Christ. The abbey church and monastery at Fulda, which he founded, and where he is buried, is today the center of German Catholicism.

By the twelfth century, the Christian sweep to Sweden was completed; Norway was won for the Church a century earlier, during the reign of King Olaf (1016-30), who later became the country's patron saint. With Ansgar, "the Apostle of the North," Denmark came into the orbit of Christendom. Mass conversions followed a consistent pattern—the people adopted the ways of kings. Greenland, Iceland and the islands off Scotland were Christianized in the path of later conquest. The conversion of the Slavs was the work of two brothers, Sts. Cyril (d. 869) and Methodius (d. 884), born in Salonika, Greece, where they received a splendid education. They mastered the Slavic language and translated the Bible into the Slavonic vernacular, which they used in the liturgy. In Rome, where Methodius was ordained a priest by Pope Adrian II (867-72), they received permission to continue to keep their sacred books in the Slavic language. Around 860 they set forth from Constantinople on a series of missions to the great Slav tribes in the mountains and plains of the north and west, and along the shores of the Black Sea. While in Rome in 869, Cyril died from a disease contracted on one of these missions and Methodius departed alone to continue their work. Despite the hostility of the German missionary priests who preached in Latin, Methodius finally became Archbishop of Moravia and devoted his last years to evangelizing the Bohemians and Poles. Nearly all the Moravian Christians united with Rome can trace their Faith back to the Church in Moravia where these men began their mission which led to the eventual conversion of millions of Slavs and the founding of a whole new Byzantine-inspired culture. Today, St. Cyril and St. Methodius are venerated in the liturgy of Catholic and Orthodox Churches alike.

IX

Charlemagne and the Holy Roman Empire

In the first eight centuries of her development, the Church not only made great spiritual gains but also grew in prominence and began to acquire temporal power. One of the rights conferred on the church by Constantine was that of owning property. During the reign of St. Sylvester I (314-35) the great basilicas of St. John Lateran, Santa Croce and St. Peter were begun. St. John Lateran, an enlargement of one of the great halls of the palace of the Laterani family, was presented to the papacy (*ca.* 311) by Constantine. As the Cathedral of Rome it still carries the proud title "Omnium Urbis et Orbis Ecclesiarum Mater et Caput" ("Mother and Head of all the churches in the city and the world"). Legend added many episodes to Pope Sylvester's association with Constantine. A spurious ninth-century document recorded the Emperor's "donation" of the city of Rome and other places in Italy and the west to Sylvester. In actuality, Constantine's gift of the Lateran Palace formed the nucleus of the "patrimony of St. Peter," the name given to the landholdings and possessions of the Holy See. Many people gave gifts and bequests, particularly their real estate, to the Church, which became one of the largest landholders in Italy. The Pope also became administrator of extensive lands in Italy, Sicily, Corsica, and even Gaul, Africa and the Orient. The income from all these properties was used by the Pope for the support of the Roman clergy, the papal court, public worship, the construction of churches, the building of shrines, and the care of the poor. With the emperors in residence at distant Constantinople and Ravenna, the Pope gradually assumed direction over many of the civic needs of Rome and became the most important employer of its people.

In 568 Italy was invaded by the Lombards and divided between Byzantine and Lombard rulers. This furnished another opportunity for the extension of papal influence. Since the exarch of Ravenna was ineffectual in the face of the Lombard threat, the Pope proved the only force to which the Romans could turn. Thus the head of the Church began to act as civil ruler. Pope Gregory the Great (590-604) pursued a peaceful policy toward the Lombards, and though rebuked many times by the Eastern Emperor, he saw his policy adopted in a peace treaty which ended the Lombard threat.

When the Merovingian line ruled France, Pepin III (d. 768), the son of Charles Martel, held the office of Mayor of the palace and for all practical purposes ruled. When his opinion was sought, Pope Zachary I (741-52) advised Pepin that the one who exercised the authority of king should bear the title. St. Boniface thereupon crowned Pepin king of the Franks.

In 750-51 the Lombards again went on a rampage which resulted in the invasion of Italy and the capture of Ravenna, from which the exarch fled. Now Rome itself was in peril. After several unsuccessful appeals to the Emperor in Constantinople for an army to protect the city, Pope Stephen III (752-57) arranged a forty-year truce, which the Lombards violated. The Pope then decided to make the long, arduous journey over the Alps to entreat Pepin's aid. Promptly agreeing to the Pope's request, the Frankish king twice led his army over the Alps, defeated the wily Lombard leader, Aistulf, and destroyed his army. Pepin then made his formal donation to the Church of Rome by giving the Pope the exarchate of Ravenna, over protests from Constantinople, the Duchy of Rome (all the land between the Apennines and the sea from Ancona to the River Po) and the states in Italy which the Lombards had invaded. In this way the Papacy secured temporal rule over the Papal States.

During the years from the reign of King Clovis to Otto, the Franks emerged as the Pope's defenders. Between 771 and 814 Pepin's son, Charlemagne, ruled the vast empire stretching from Saxony to Italy, from the Atlantic to Slavic lands. It was this great warrior-ruler who once again led his Frankish armies into Italy, defeating the Lombards at Pavia and saving Rome from invasion. While his troops still battled the Lombards, Charlemagne went to Rome to attend a conference wherein Pope Adrian I (772-95) formally asked the king to confirm Pepin's gift of land. Not only did Charlemagne affix his signature to the official document presented, but he added more territory to the gift of his father. As a result of these gifts and the protection provided by Pepin and Charlemagne, the temporal sovereignty of the Popes was established.

Pope Leo III (795-816), the saintly and zealous successor of Pope Adrian, was the victim of a series of conspiracies by his enemies which reached a low point in the Pontiff's seizure and imprisonment. Charlemagne presided over a second assembly in Rome, which resulted in the complete vindication of Leo III (it was shown that the accusations made against him were false) and the banishment of his enemies. After this Charlemagne and his nobles remained in Rome to protect the Pope. This newly developed alliance between Pope and Emperor reached a climax when, on Christmas morning, in the year 800 Pope Leo crowned Charlemagne while he knelt in prayer at the tomb of St. Peter. The chronicler Einhard relates that his coronation took Charlemagne by surprise, but he accepted both the crown and the title of Roman Emperor. Thus was reborn the Western Roman Empire, no longer pagan but Christian. This was one of the most important events of the Middle Ages. The Byzantine emperors hereafter exercised no real authority in the West. Heresies had sapped their strength, whereas the Franks proved effective rulers of the West, and performed many distinguished services for Christendom. Charlemagne, in fostering the spread of the Catholic religion, proceeded violently in forcing baptism on heathens, as among the Saxons. That his tactics are repugnant to modern sentiment cannot be denied, but we must also add that the Saxons embraced with especial ardor the religion which in the beginning was forced on them.[10]

The term "Holy Roman Empire" was later used with the imperial title during the time of Frederick I (1152-1190), an outgrowth of popular usage and old Roman custom. The Holy Roman Empire was designed to provide the perfect example of what is meant by the union of church and state. As time proved, events made it extremely difficult to maintain a harmonious relationship but in theory at least the Holy Roman Empire came into being to advance St. Augustine's conception of the ideal Christian community as set forth in *The City of God*.[11]

Some think Charlemagne intended to reverse what Constantine had done—and make Rome the capital once more of the Empire. Whatever his intention, if

the age before was dark, now came the dawn of the
Carolingian Renaissance of the ninth century. The
Emperor at Constantinople of course refused to relinquish his claims in the West and consequently
throughout the Middle Ages there were two emperors
and two empires in the East and West. Charlemagne
continued as the most important ruler in the West,
guardian of the church and patron of education, bring-
ing to his court at Aachen the most distinguished
scholars he could find, founding monasteries, and
establishing parish schools. The most famous of these
was the palace school over which Alcuin, an Anglo-
Saxon cleric, took charge. He was a teacher of unusual ability who translated the truths of science and
literature into terms readily understood by his pupils.
Even Charlemagne, who could do little more than
write his own name, was tutored by Alcuin. Thus was
initiated a revival of learning, the real beginning of
intellectual progress which was to carry over into the
reigns of Charlemagne's successors.

Unfortunately, Charlemagne's son, Louis the Pious,
though a conscientious ruler, was a political dwarf in
comparison with his father and was unable to combat
the rivalries and revolts of his sons, the discord in civil
and ecclesiastical life and the attacks of Mohammedans,
Norsemen and Slavs. The division of the Empire among
his sons, of whom none but Louis survived his father's
death, was a grave mistake. Disintegration and further
division followed until the once proud Empire of
Charlemagne was broken up into some fifty smaller
principalities. Feudal society and its accompanying
chaos filled the vacuum left by the collapse of Carolingian supremacy. Power became localized; the lay
or spiritual nobles were the real rulers, even of Rome
itself. The ascendancy of the Capet family in France

removed that country from the Empire; thereafter, the recently converted Saxon rulers and people from the non-Roman East became the source of imperial power, with Italy never permanently independent of the German emperors.

During all the turmoil and tribulation which ensued, the Church tried to assert her holiness through the state, and through it all the Church remained the most vigorous influence for civilization in Western Europe. Church government preserved the traditions of unity and central authority which had been the glory of imperial Rome, and Christian teaching inspired all efforts at reform.

X

The Eastern Schism

Ever since the time when the capital of the Empire was removed from Rome to Constantinople, the East and West had drifted further apart. Constantinople's fortunes rose as Rome's glories vanished. At the end of the sixth century one patriarch of the New Rome tried to assume the title of "Universal Patriarch." This prompted Gregory the Great to defend the primacy of the Pope. As a result of this and the Papacy's increasing involvement in Western political affairs, some Eastern patriarchs developed a dislike for Rome. Moreover, the Eastern emperors continued to practice Caesaropapism, that is, to meddle in church affairs.

An outstanding example of Caesaropapism is found in the iconoclastic controversy. This struggle involved repeated excommunications of Eastern Emperors by Popes over a long period of time. The point at issue—the use of images—was a deep-seated tradition in the East and West. Many persons in court and intellectual circles felt that the monasteries had become centers of idolatrous image worship. The crisis came when the Eastern Emperor, Leo III (717-40), forbade all representations of human beings in religious art. He even commanded Pope Gregory II (715-31) to accept the edict. This resulted in the destruction of many of the Church's greatest works of art, the persecution of their defenders, the secularization of the monasteries and the enforced exile of thousands of artists, monks and priests to Italy and Northern Europe. This controversy did much to harm the unity of the still undivided Church. In 787 the seventh ecumenical council at Nicaea defined that "both the figure of the sacred and life-giving cross, as also the venerable and holy images . . . are to be placed suitably. in the holy churches of God . . ." but that the honor paid to them is only relative for the sake of their prototypes: they are to receive veneration, not adoration. That is the belief of the Catholic Church and of the now separated Orthodox Church. But in 814 iconoclasm broke out again at the instigation of the Emperor Leo the Armenian and his successors. The persecution of Catholics and the destruction of monasteries and images lasted until the Empress Theodora became regent in 842. St. John the Damascene and St. Theodore the Studite were the principal defenders of the Orthodox teaching and practice concerning images. The Eastern custom of using icons and mosaics but no round statues or other carved images seems to be an outgrowth of the iconoclastic controversy.

These disturbances in East-West relations were important in themselves but no one of them was sufficiently powerful to create the permanent religious break between Rome and the East which is known in history as the Great Schism. In the ninth century the Photian schism brought East and West into formal conflict. Photius, Byzantium's greatest lay scholar, was selected by the Eastern Emperor, Michael III, to succeed the banished St. Ignatius as Patriarch of Constantinople. Church law prohibited the election of laymen to a patriarchate, especially consecration by a deposed bishop. Therefore Pope St. Nicholas I (858-67) excommunicated Photius in 863. Outraged, Photius in turn excommunicated the whole Latin Church and declared Pope Nicholas deposed in 867.

A period of charges and countercharges followed during which Michael was assassinated, Photius deposed, Ignatius reinstated and, after his death, Photius was again restored as Patriarch after asking pardon from Pope John VIII (872-82) for past offenses. But Photius continued to oppose the authority and teaching of the Church until his final removal in 886.

A century or more of outward peace between Greeks and Romans followed, but the fires of discord flared up again after Michael Caerularius was consecrated Patriarch of Constantinople (1043-58). All the old antagonisms and prejudices that Photius had presented in his long list of charges against Rome were revived by Caerularius: condemnation of the Saturday fast, the use of dairy foods during Lent, celibacy among the clergy, the use of *filioque* in the Nicene Creed, and the use of unleavened bread in the Eucharistic Sacrament. Altogether there were thirty-three objections. The final blow came when Michael ordered the closing of all Latin monasteries and churches in Constantinople. All Latin priests were ordered to adopt the Greek rite and those who refused were excommunicated. It is said that Michael's chancellor scattered the Holy Eucharist of unleavened bread in the city streets.

Pope Leo IX (1049-54) protested vigorously and urged respect for the practices of the Roman Church which had originated with St. Peter. For a time it seemed as if a peaceful settlement would be reached, but at the crucial point when the papal legates were en route to Constantinople to adjust the differences with emperor and patriarch, Pope Leo died.

The papal legates were arrogant and unyielding; they handled the situation badly. Michael Caerularius, for his part, was insolent. The consultations thus deteriorated and were finally pronounced a failure. The climax came during that fateful hour when the Roman legates entered the great cathedral of Santa Sophia, declared Michael Caerularius *anathema* and placed the official documents of excommunication on the high altar. It is possible that the excommunication was canonically invalid, owing to Pope Leo's recent death. In any case, it was directed only against Caerularius, and two of his prelates. The Byzantine Church as a whole and the other Eastern patriarchs were not (and never have been) excommunicated. But this event increased the separatist tendency of the Orthodox Eastern Church, which gradually grew and hardened after 1054, becoming finally official when Constantinople repudiated the Union of Florence in 1472.

Like Photius before him, Michael retaliated by holding a council of his own in 1054 and excommunicating the Pope. Thus was brought into existence the Greek Orthodox Church, which has never since recognized the authority of Rome. At the time it occurred, the division was thought to be only temporary but it proved permanent. It is a sad, even a tragic commentary to note that the Church of Constantinople and Byzantium virtually separated itself from Rome.

XI

The Dark Days of the Papacy

Out of the breakup of Charlemagne's Holy Roman
Empire developed the feudal system. In the years of
chaos and unrest that followed, the Moslems renewed
their aggression in Spain and the savage, anti-Christian
tribes of Denmark harassed England and the continent. In Spain these ravages produced martyrs like
St. Eulogius of Cordoba and the Bishop of Toledo,
beheaded in 859. Most of the great Spanish churches
were turned into mosques. Scattered groups of Christians like those at Saragossa continued to practice their
religion. Barcelona was restored to Christianity by 801
and Aragon, with its famed abbey of Montserrat con-
taining the shrine of the Black Virgin, became an important Christian center.

Alfred of England saved half his kingdom by con-
fining the invaders to the Danelaw, and the Danish
siege of Paris in 888 was frustrated by the French
victory at Louvain (891). These events left Western
Europe the scene of immense destruction, waste and
chaos. Discipline, by the late 900's, had grown lax.
A series of scandals disgraced the Papacy for over
a hundred years, partly as a result of lay domination
over the election of Popes and the stranglehold an
unruly and barbarous baronage kept over the Papal
State. Moreover, the Church was weakened by immorality, pluralism, ignorance, simony and nepotism.

The clergy was subject to lay control. From the murder of Pope John VIII in 882 to 1046 there were in a hundred and sixty years thirty-seven Popes. Many of them were honest and worthy of the chair of Peter, but many of them met violent deaths at the hands of their enemies. Nevertheless, a ninth-century Pope, St. Nicholas I (858-67), is one of the three to whom posterity has given the name of "the Great." He played a masterly role in the affair of Photius, and courageously refused, despite threats and an invasion of his States, to acknowledge the divorce of Lothair, king of Lorraine (863).[12]

When the house of Theophylact gained power over affairs in Rome, they laid violent hands on the Holy See and for the next seventy years they appointed Popes of their choice, resulting in the scandals proceeding from the rule of the really "bad Popes" who have been the source of so much controversy.

During this period a group of shameless women ruled Rome. Marozia, the daughter of Theodora, who had herself called "Madame Senator," was influential in raising Pope John X (914-28) to the See of Peter. A genius in military leadership, John X formed an Confederation of Italian princes and rode at the head of their armies in the campaign against the Saracens, whose defeat ended a great danger to Italy. At that time the papal military government was housed on the Palatine Hill in the old palace of the Caesars, and ecclesiastical administration was conducted in the Lateran Palace of the Popes, the gift of Constantine. Marozia eventually turned against Pope John X, an able churchman. In the uprising provoked by her, the papal palace was invaded, John's brother killed and the Pope imprisoned. His death, shortly after, was reportedly caused by suffocation. During the reign of Marozia's son, Alberic, the Popes were only nominal civil rulers of the Papal State.

After the Carolingian period the political center of Europe shifted from France to Germany and halfway through the tenth century the Germans produced a great king, Otto I (936-73). Although he was looked upon by the Byzantine Emperor as a usurper, Otto the Great unified the German tribes, gave them a sense of national life, and made them a powerful political body. He ended the Magyar threat, defeated the Danes and Slavs, crossed the Alps and in 951 marched into Italy and made himself king. Pope John XII (955-64) sought Otto's aid against the king's representative in Italy. Otto responded quickly and amid great splendor Pope John crowned him Holy Roman Emperor, thus reviving the empire of Charlemagne. Otto promised to return all lands belonging to the Church, and John swore he would render no assistance to the Emperor's enemies, but faithless as he was, John formed an alliance with Otto's enemies. This prompted the Emperor to lay siege to Rome and for the remaining years of his reign Otto retained strict control over Rome and the papal elections. He tried, nominated and on occasion deposed Popes. Reform was thus entirely at the mercy of lay support.

Henry III of Germany invaded Italy in 1046 and put an end to papal scandals. He ousted all claimants and brought about the naming of German Popes. At the synod of Sutri, Clement II (1046-47) was chosen Pope at Henry's suggestion. Imperial support for the Papacy would not have been enough, but the third German Pope was Leo IX (1049-1054), a man of remarkable ability, aided by the equally capable young monk, Hildebrand, from the abbey of Cluny. Together they formed a party of reform in Rome. This party, later led by Hildebrand, and aided by the military strength of the Normans, succeeded in freeing the Papacy from dependence on any secular power and enabled the Pope to assert such effective control over Europe through the full use of his spiritual authority that never again during the Middle Ages could secular princes exercise unchallenged authority over the Papacy. An end came to the dark, disgraceful days in Rome, which gave way to the High Middle Ages.

The weakness of the Papacy to the end of the eleventh century was accompanied by the growth of the monastic system in isolated feudal units. During the tenth century there was a great reform movement associated with the monastery of Cluny—and with the successful local efforts of such prelates as St. Dunstan (d. 988), a pioneer in religious reforms, the Abbot of Glastonbury, Archbishop of Canterbury and the real ruler of England.

Regarded next to Rome as the ecclesiastical capital of Europe, the abbey of Cluny, near Mâcon (fifty miles north of Lyons) was founded in 910 by Duke William I of Aquitaine. The terms of its charter provided that the Benedictine rule had to be observed in letter and spirit, the monks were to select their own abbot and both monks and abbot were to be subject not to any lay ruler but to the Pope alone.[13] Thus began a movement of world-wide significance, inaugurating a new form of Benedictine life with a highly centralized government and freedom from secular control which enabled the new monastery to pursue a program of religious reform unhindered by feudal obligations.

The congregation of Cluny took form under a number of competent and saintly abbots. Cluniac monks were appointed papal officials (cardinals, legates, bishops, e.g.) and many were elected to the Papacy itself during the eleventh and twelfth centuries. A few Cluniac Popes were Urban II, Urban V and Paschal II. Under the guidance of Abbot St. Odo (927) the great struggle for reform which was destined to affect Rome itself commenced.

Daily life under the Cluniac abbot (Berno of Gigny was selected as the first ruler) was grounded on the principle that the Divine Office is almost the only work for monks; church services were multiplied and carried out with much ritual and splendor. Thus at Cluny there was an extraordinary amount of praying, and little time was left for study. The Cistercians later criticized the Cluniacs for merely praying and not working, but they really prayed, and the people had confidence in their prayers. They especially fostered prayers for the dead; these, and their generosity to the poor, were sources of their wealth. In 998 Abbot St. Odilo introduced the commemoration of the dead on All Souls' Day, which in 1030 was fixed as November 2.

The reforms brought about by the Cluniac order brought a new spirituality during the tenth century. St. Odo was commissioned by the Pope to rehabilitate the monasteries of Gaul and Italy; in this way a large number of abbeys throughout Europe combined under Cluniac jurisdiction to form a great feudal organization. By the twelfth century the abbot of Cluny was head of some three hundred monasteries; by the fifteenth century the number had increased to eight hundred. These figures go far to explain why Cluny was such a vital force in the next three centuries. Some writers believe the contribution of Cluny to the reform movement has been perhaps exaggerated but initial inspiration undoubtedly came from the lives and teachings of the monks attached to that abbey and its subsidiaries. The reform flourished for 250 years; then it declined quickly. Studies, teaching, manual labor almost disappeared, and Cluny itself, with its gigantic Romanesque basilica, was destroyed in the French Revolution.

During the short reign of Pope Nicholas II (1059-61) an important change was made in the procedure of papal elections. Formerly the Pope was chosen by the clergy and people of Rome. Christian emperors had often influenced this choice and they also intervened in the affairs of the city of Rome. In an effort to end political intrigues and factional domination of the Papacy, the Lateran Council of 1059 decreed that the right of choosing the Pope belongs to the cardinals alone—those priests living in the city of Rome, who performed the key functions in the administration of the Church—and all new Popes must be chosen from the Roman clergy. Thus a significant step was taken in the regulation of papal elections. The role of the emperor was limited to the vague right of "interference." Not until the reign of Pius X (1903-14) was the intervention of secular power formally prohibited.

From the monasteries and cloisters came the stimulus by which Europe learned to build and carve again. The monks themselves were at first the chief workers and builders although lay workers were used for major projects. The appearance of so many impressive new structures was a symbol of the Church's increased wealth and power. Many of the large monastery churches were on pilgrimage routes. Pilgrims, impelled by the fervor of the time, would come from all over Europe to pay their respects at a shrine holding relics of an important saint. The chief roads led to Rome, to the tomb of St. Peter; to Paris, where St. Louis IX built that gem, La Ste.-Chapelle, with its repository for the Holy thorn from Our Lord's crown; to Santiago de

Compostela in southern Spain, with the grave of St. James the Great; and finally, to the Holy Sepulcher in Jerusalem. The pilgrims were housed overnight in the monasteries (for there were few cities and towns, and no inns). Free will offerings were made for the hospitality received. In this way the monasteries accumulated considerable wealth. The pilgrim routes in turn became the leading trade routes of medieval commerce.

The Germans made ivory carving an important feature of religious art. The tenth century "Doubting Thomas" demonstrates the high emotional level reached in a representation such as this, where the saint literally climbs upward into the wounds of the Lord.

The monk, Hildebrand, continued to work diligently at the death of each Pope for the election of a worthy successor, and the reform movement gathered momentum under his firm hand. A Protestant writer called his success "the victory of the unarmed monk." The time finally came—at the close of the funeral services for Pope Alexander II (1061-73) in St. John Lateran —when the voices of clergy and people mingled in cries demanding the selection of Hildebrand as the new Pope. The cardinals gathered in great haste at the Church of St. Peter in Chains and being of one mind with the people of Rome, Hildebrand became Pope Gregory VII—and the curtain was about to rise on one of the most dramatic periods in Church history.

XII

Gregory VII and His Age

One of the most important features of feudalism was the lord's right of appointment. This right included, by the tenth century, the exercise by a noble of a voice in the appointment of the priest who was to be pastor and live on his property or the naming of the abbot of a monastery whose lands were his gift. It was not long before nobles and kings extended this so-called right of "lay investiture" to the cathedrals served by bishops, and considered themselves owners of the diocese. When a king or noble secured the appointment of his candidate to a church office, it was customary during the Middle Ages for all transfers of property and appointments to be carried out in a symbolic feudal ceremony in which, for example, the appointee to a bishopric received from the hands of his overlord, whether he be king, emperor or noble, the episcopal staff (crozier) and ring, the signs of his spiritual office symbolizing his role as shepherd of the flock. He also received whatever titles, possessions and temporal rights went with the office. In a separate ceremony, the bishop was consecrated by another bishop; cardinals received the red hat. No appointment was valid until the act of papal consecration had been performed. As evil as the abuses of lay investiture became, no attempt was made by lay lords to confer the power of orders, or consecration.

Not only did the misuse of the power of lay investiture lead to bad appointments to sees and prelacies by lay nobles and princes, but it also led to other abuses, such as keeping the sees vacant and simony (the buying and selling of sacred objects and appointments). Although the law of the Church had required celibacy of the clergy since the fourth century, the law was largely disregarded in the ninth and tenth centuries, during which some bishops, abbots and priests raised large families, provided for and endowed them with the lands and revenues of the Church.

At the Synod of 1074 Pope St. Gregory (1073-85) launched his first attack against simony: anyone guilty of this abuse was barred from performing the work of a Church Office. Anyone found to have secured an appointment in return for money lost the office. The people were not permitted to attend Church ceremonies conducted by anyone who flouted these laws and finally those who violated the obligation of celibacy were suspended from clerical office. These laws were intended by Gregory to root out the two great abuses of simony and marriage of the clergy. Above all, however, he considered lay control of the Church the greatest abuse and the root of all evil. This meant by necessity the removal from the hands of kings, emperors and nobles of the selection of priests, bishops and archbishops. He wanted to strike at the more deadly abuse of usurping the papal appointive power, and to free the Church from lay control. The opportunity soon presented itself.

The controversy over investiture between the Popes and bishops on one side, and the kings of Germany, France and England on the other, lasted from 1074 to 1122. The young German Emperor, Henry IV (1056-1106), at first asserted he would observe the urgently repeated prohibition of lay investiture. However, Henry resisted the papal reforms to stamp out simony, clerical incontinence and lay investiture. In 1075, without consulting the Pope, he named a new archbishop for Milan (no prince of the empire as, for example, the archbishop of Mainz). This was a clear invasion of the spiritual realm and a challenge to papal authority. Gregory VII sent Henry a sharp note and threatened excommunication. In reply, the rash, headstrong King gathered twenty-six bishops at Worms in 1076 and declared Gregory "deposed." He wrote an insulting letter to "the pseudo monk, Hildebrand," upon receipt of which Pope Gregory excommunicated Henry IV and released his subjects from their obedience to him.

While the act of Gregory VII stunned the nobles of Germany and Europe, it was not unprecedented.[14] Henry IV was expected to take up arms against the Pope but war did not ensue immediately for the majority of German bishops withdrew their allegiance to Henry, while the lay princes and papal legates decided he should be tried by Gregory at a Council in Augsburg in 1077. Until then Henry was to remain in retirement, abstaining from government. In the event that within a year he was not loosed from the ban of excommunication, he would be forced to give up the crown.

In evident apprehension of his impending downfall, Henry with an armed force crossed the Alps amid the cold of a terrible winter as Gregory was proceeding with his retinue into North Italy, where he was to await the German escort which would accompany him across the Alps and into Augsburg. While awaiting this escort, Gregory withdrew into the Apennines to the strongly fortified castle of Canossa (between Modena and Parma), which was the property of the loyal Countess Matilda of Tuscany. Henry made no attack, but instead dispatched humble letters to Canossa in which he promised to submit to all Gregory's demands. Then the Emperor appeared in person and stationed himself outside the castle gates for three days in the cold and snow, dressed in the garb of a penitent, entreating a papal audience and forgiveness. As a priest, Gregory VII could not refuse to receive him and to grant absolution to a sinner who asked pardon with all the signs of true remorse. Henry promised and swore to do all that the Pope demanded, and the Pope lifted the ban of excommunication.

This incident of Emperor Henry IV at Canossa has been more celebrated in history than it deserves to be. It has become symbolic of the triumph of the Church over the state during the High Middle Ages, but in fact the whole dramatic episode was a clever dodge of the Emperor-elect whereby, coming as a penitent, he avoided the deposition which would have followed his continued excommunication. As if in proof of his craftiness, Henry soon after violated his promises and returned to the forbidden practice of lay investiture. Gregory renewed the ban of excommunication in 1080. Civil war followed in Germany, where a rival emperor was set up. Henry's faction invaded Italy, marched on Rome and Gregory sought refuge in the impregnable castle of Sant' Angelo, while Henry mastered Rome and set up a rival Pope, Clement, who in turn crowned him emperor. In 1084, Robert of Guiscard, Gregory's ally who had been away fighting the Greeks in Illyria, arrived with an army of Normans and Saracens, drove out Henry IV, sacked Rome and freed the Pope.

Unfortunately, the liberators so outraged the Roman populace with their destruction and rapaciousness that the people now turned against Gregory VII. The Norman troops conducted the aging Pontiff to safe quarters, first at Monte Cassino and then at Salerno, where he became ill and died in 1085. On his deathbed, the former Cluniac monk reviewed to attending cardinals the great principles which had regulated his life. He paraphrased the words of the forty-fourth psalm—"I have loved justice and hated iniquity," but instead of continuing, "therefore hath God anointed me with the oil of gladness," he ended with the plaintive sentence, "therefore I die in exile." His belief in the justice of his cause remained unshaken, and the bishops of Rome have never departed from the main principles laid down by him. It may be that he accomplished more as Hildebrand than as Gregory VII but he was unquestionably the very soul of reform.

Henry IV died in 1106, a lonely, defeated man. His son, Henry V, was a worse emperor than his father but he at least saw the wisdom, by 1122, of coming to terms with Pope Callistus II (1119-24) on the question of lay investiture. In the Concordat of Worms, the Emperor promised to relinquish the right to confer the signs of spiritual office (the ring and staff); he also promised to allow free elections. In return, the Pope permitted the Emperor to attend an election and confer the signs of temporal power after the election and consecration had taken place. Although other disputes were to follow, the Concordat of Worms showed that a solution was at least possible.

The papalists, who refused to recognize the anti-Pope Clement, found a new leader as uncompromising as Gregory in Urban II, whom they elected to the Papacy in 1088. The Emperor, Henry IV, had been too deeply involved in ceaseless struggles with his German rebels, among whom was numbered his oldest son and heir, Conrad, to take decisive measures in Italy; and then an opportunity was offered to Urban, which he grasped.

XIII

The Crusades

After the year 1000 the Church entered upon a great revival. Step by step Western Christendom mounted to the apex of medieval civilization, developing a philosophy, architecture, literature and art of its own and even establishing a Latin kingdom in the heart of Islam. Of all the memorable phenomena of life in the Middle Ages, no two stand out more strongly than the Crusades and the Gothic Cathedral, the latter being the symbol of a creative, intelligent and highly imaginative drive toward the supernatural, and the former its active form, the self-sacrificing desire to gain a touch of sanctity by rescuing the Holy Land from the infidels (not without a bit of booty along the way).[15]

Christian pilgrimages to the Holy Land during these decades became increasingly imperiled, for while the Saracens, who had conquered Palestine in the seventh century, had adopted a moderate policy, and merely subjected Christians to special taxation, the routes eastward and the holy places were from the eleventh century controlled by the more uncompromising Seljuk Turks, who launched barbaric persecutions of the Christians from time to time. Western Europe was thus prompted to take the initiative against its old enemy, the Moslems. The first aim, under the leadership of the commercial Italian cities, was to break Moslem sea power in the Mediterranean.

Another important factor in the course of events was supplied by Byzantium. In 1081, an able and astute emperor, Alexius Comnenus, assumed the diadem at Constantinople. The armies of the Eastern Empire had gone down in bitter defeat before the Seljuk Turks in 1071 when Syria and parts of Asia Minor had been torn away from Byzantine allegiance. Though the Church of Byzantium was in schism with the Holy See from 1054, Alexius now appealed for aid from the West to recover his lost dominions. Conditions were more favorable at this time for papal action. The West cared very little for Byzantium's lost territories, but in an inspiring age of faith it could rise to the idea of a Holy War against the infidel which might wrest the Holy Land from the Turks, win the Eastern Church to reunion with Rome and direct warring Europe under papal guidance toward a new and consecrated cause.

A great Council of the Church was therefore summoned in 1095 at Clermont. At the height of the lay investiture quarrel a vast number of bishops, abbots, nobles and knights (forming a crowd estimated at 100,000) assembled in an atmosphere of fervent emotion to discuss church reform and the troublesome Henry with Pope Urban II. This vigorous, shrewd, French-born Pope, a former abbot of Cluny, who so forcefully opposed Henry IV (whose troops were then occupying Rome and supporting an anti-Pope), was one of the most popular of medieval pontiffs even though he was for some time a Pope without a see. At Clermont he delivered one of the most stirring discourses of all time, describing the desecration of the holy places and the suffering of Christians. Was Jerusalem to remain in the hands of the infidel? he asked. The reply was not an answer but a command: "Men of God, men chosen and blessed among all, combine your forces. Take the road to the Holy Sepulcher assured of the imperishable glory that awaits you in God's kingdom. Let each one deny himself and take the Cross!" As Urban made his final fervid appeal, the universal cry rang out: "*Deus vult!*" (Good wills it!"). The First Crusade was launched.

The cross, painted on the right shoulder of the knight's tunic, was the symbol of the campaigns. By evening of that same day there was no more red paint or red cloth to be had in Clermont. As popular preachers echoed the appeal of Urban the movement spread across Europe. Indulgences, protection of family and property and a special blessing were granted by the Church to those who undertook the long journey.

The first wave of Crusaders, under Peter the Hermit, who posed as a pilgrim from Jerusalem without ever having been there, and Walter the Penniless consisted of ill-armed enthusiasts, who asked of each town along the way: "Is that Jerusalem?" They were frightfully massacred by the Turks; not one of them reached the goal. But in 1096, four great feudal armies, whose knights came largely from France, England, the Lowlands and Norman Italy, taking four different routes, assembled at Constantinople and were ferried across to Asia Minor the following spring. Nicaea, Antioch and Edessa were taken and converted into Christian states. Under heavy armor, in unbelievable heat, through terrible marches across the desert north of the Holy Land, decimated by plague and malnutrition, the army of Crusaders at last reached Jerusalem in June, 1099, three years after leaving their bases in Europe. Ending a five-week siege, they hurled themselves upon the Holy City. So hideous was the slaughter that even the Franks were afterward ashamed. As the sun's rays faded over David's gates, the conquerors put away their weapons and armor. Barefooted and washed of blood, in clean mantles and calmed of their insane fury, they climbed the Via Dolorosa "sighing and weeping, through the Holy Place of the city where Jesus Christ the Saviour of the world had trodden . . . then gently kissed the spots on which His feet had stood." Raymond the Chaplain wrote: ". . . we had then the reward of all our labor when we beheld the devotion of the pilgrims at the Sepulcher of the Lord."

Two weeks later the Latin kingdom of Jerusalem was born, with Godfrey of Bouillon as its uncrowned ruler (he refused to wear a crown of gold in the city where his Savior had worn a crown of thorns). Before the glad tidings reached the city of Rome, Urban II died. Upon his tomb were placed these words:

Urbanus Secundus
Auctor Expeditionis in Infideles

Other kingdoms were founded along feudal lines, at Edessa, Tripoli, Galilee and Lesser Armenia. A constant stream of Crusaders continued to arrive in the East to bolster the new states. A unique institution, the military orders, the most famous of them being the Knights Hospitalers and the Knights Templars, were founded to care for the sick and wounded and to protect the Holy Land, but operations were continuously hampered by lack of funds. Asia Minor was still held by the Moslems, who constantly raided the Christian strongholds in the East. The Latin kingdom survived nearly two hundred years, almost constantly at war not only with the Moslems but even with the Byzantines (Byzantium's policy was to keep the Latins weak) and its own European allies. Gradually the Moslems won back the entire Christian territory north of the

Kingdom of Jerusalem during the twelfth century. The Moslems, unlike the Christians, were now united under a brilliant statesman and military chieftain named Saladin. So remarkable a leader was he that he became the personal friend of King Richard the Lion-Hearted. Dante put him in that special part of Hell—"the circle of the Righteous Pagans"—where the souls are gathered whose single sorrow it is not to have known Jesus. Before long Saladin had recaptured Jerusalem, and once again the Holy City became a Moslem citadel.

Realizing that halfhearted measures would never bring success in the Holy Land, Pope Clement III ordered a tax on all income and asked the three most powerful rulers of Europe to take the Cross. They were Frederick Barbarossa of Germany, Philip Augustus of France and Henry II of England (succeeded by his son, Richard the Lion-Hearted). Frederick Barbarossa (Red Beard) was the Holy Roman Emperor. Though he had been in constant conflict with the Papacy, Frederick was enough of a Christian to be outraged by Saladin's victories and to place himself and his armies under Pope Clement for the Third Crusade. Seizing the initiative from the other two kings, Frederick rolled up a string of victories as Saladin retreated. But Moslem luck turned when Barbarossa suffered a stroke while bathing in an icy stream—the river Saleph in Asia Minor—and died. After the other two kings decided to join forces to take Acre, Philip deserted and Richard attempted to carry on alone. The most he could secure was a treaty from Saladin promising free access by Christians to the Holy Places. In a short time the situation was as bad as before.

Denouncing Europe's rulers as selfish men "less willing to suffer for Christ than was Christ for them," Pope Innocent III proclaimed a Fourth Crusade, ordered public prayers for its success, forbade wars between Christians and taxed everyone, including the cardinals and himself, to raise funds for the armies. An overland route to the Middle East was ruled out. The crafty Venetian merchants offered their ships for half the territory conquered and 85,900 gold marks. Because only part of the money was delivered they marooned the Crusaders on an island until they promised to destroy Zara, Venice's rival city on the Adriatic. Furious when he heard of the sacking of Zara, Innocent excommunicated the Venetian leaders but after he lifted the ban the expedition continued on its way to Constantinople, another of Venice's rivals, and when the Crusaders saw the mighty prize before them, a chronicler tells us, "no man there was of such hardihood but that his flesh trembled." In 1204, Constantinople was taken. A year later riots gave the pretext for a three-day sacking of the city during which even the churches were desecrated. Soon loot from the Byzantine Empire decorated all Europe. Venice's famous bronze doors, which stand before St. Mark's, were taken from Constantine's Hippodrome. Troops that should have garrisoned the Holy Land were diverted to serve the Latin Kingdom of Byzantium.

Two Children's Crusades followed, with the expectation of achieving by innocence what grown men had failed to achieve by brute force, but these also ended disastrously. Finally, in Louis IX of France, one of the Church's greatest saints, reappeared all the fervor, sanctity, integrity and spirit that had inspired the First Crusade. Alone among all the nobles to be persuaded to undertake still another venture into the Holy Land, he succeeded first in capturing Damietta but delayed too long in pursuing the enemy. Then Louis fell sick. His army was routed by the Turks and he was captured while lying feverish in a hut. For four more years, after he was ransomed, Louis ruled the Latin kingdom and then returned to France to plan another Crusade. This last Crusade (1270) foolishly headed for North Africa, however, instead of the Holy Land. Louis fell ill once again of fever and died August 25, 1270. The Crusades were over.

XIV

The Age of Faith

Conditions during the early days of feudalism, after the barbarian invasions, were not very conducive to the development of culture and art. There had been periods, as during the reign of Charlemagne and later, of Otto the Great, when cultural gains were real. Gradually, these periods of revival became more frequent and by the end of the eleventh century Western Christendom was on the road to restoration. During the High Middle Ages of the twelfth and thirteenth centuries, European civilization entered upon a cultural flowering which took many forms.

One of them is evidenced in the great crusading expeditions against the Moslems in the Near East; this represented the most active form taken by aspirations to sanctity. Among practical considerations marked during this period of growth were the expansion of commerce, the growth of cities, the extension of agriculture and a great revival in the monasteries. During this time, the Catholic Church, which was central in Western European development, secured a strong papal monarchy, sponsored new religious orders, fought courageously against heresy, renewed the struggle with the secular princes, founded new universities and a new Christian theology.

Of all the phenomena which characterized life in this remarkable age nothing is so symbolic of its creative, intelligent and highly imaginative drive toward the supernatural as the climax reached in medieval Gothic architecture. The Gothic cathedral constituted the fullest expression of the newly found freedom of the era. Standing on one side of the market place, the cathedral became the physical and spiritual focus of town life. Daily, townspeople gathered in it for worship. Mystery plays were performed on its steps; wandering preachers gave their sermons in its shadow. In its fine, traceried sculpture and richly colored stained-glass windows, the knowledge of an age was summarized for an illiterate people.

> The cathedral, the symbol of the universal church, dominated not only the town but the aesthetics of the time as well. Through the triumph of logic, the Gothic builder produced a thrilling and inspiring religious structure in which the immense, sometimes invisible heights of the vaults, vibrating with the color of stained glass, and the rich music [of Gregorian chant] unite to achieve a more effective act of faith.[16]

The twelfth-century Gothic structures which arose in France represent an entirely new approach to church building. The term "Gothic" was applied during the Renaissance to this architecture as a symbol of barbarism. The Romanesque style aimed at producing an open skeleton of stone, supporting stone vaulting. Using newly discovered principles of elasticity and equilibrium, thrust and counterthrust, medieval Gothic builders achieved greater height and lightness of appearance. Their characteristic pointed arches permitted this and also more flexibility in building. The intellectually responsible workmen and builders attempted effects increasingly audacious—not without some failures: part of the Amiens cathedral collapsed in 1284 because the piers were not substantial enough and the vaulting too delicate. Through the military activity of Roman barons and the movement of merchants and artists, the Gothic idea was diffused over all of Europe. Other countries, like England, Germany and Spain, produced modified versions, drawing upon France's inspired achievements.

Gothic stained glass, which was decorative in its application of color areas tied together by pieces of lead and stone tracery, replaced the former Romanesque wall paintings. Far more light was admitted through these immense, translucent windows. The brightness is distinctly muted, however, as it passes through small units of roughly blown colored glass. It is a rich, full light which "conveys a spiritual feeling." Subdued color radiance does not always reach the tops of the vaults for it is sometimes obscured in velvety shadows, "adding to the sense of infinitude and mystical aspirations existing in an atmosphere created by the many-toned, vibrating luminosity." The Gothic glassmakers even utilized the changing quality of natural light, which moves from the red to the violet side of the spectrum during daytime. The windows in the apse (east) end are dominantly red in tone, while the rose wheel over the entrance, or the west end, may be violet-hued, so the sunlight can reinforce each window as it moves from one end of the cathedral to the other.[17] Historians tell us that medieval man recognized the meaning of these stone and glass decorations for which later generations use guidebooks.

Acknowledged everywhere as the Gothic masterpiece of the twelfth century is Chartres Cathedral. Perhaps more than any other French cathedral this one approaches perfection with its wonderful proportions, exquisite ornamental sculptural accompaniments and upward-sweeping towers.

When fire destroyed the original building in 1194 a vast migration of French pilgrims headed for the episcopal See of Chartres to rebuild for the Blessed Virgin a suitable place of refuge. Even cripples and the sick trailed along to pray while the others worked. In their self-organized community, which was really a city of tents around Chartres, the workers elected their leaders who in turn were supervised by monks. Everyone worked under the direction of the unknown genius who designed the cathedral and supervised the building. Work progressed rapidly in a spirit of sacrifice, penance and high enthusiasm. The cathedral was dedicated in 1260.

While Gothic was the architectural style of the age, the more individual art of painting also entered on a glorious era. St. Francis of Assisi is often called the father of Italian art, and with a certain elasticity of meaning this is true. For he and Dominic certainly rejuvenated and reanimated church art. After Giotto, who led the Renaissance in Italian painting, came the incomparable Fra Angelico, a more natural and realistic painter than his predecessors. But the new artists were still medieval and profoundly religious. They did not depart from the Gothic style and were the recognized interpreters of Christian truth.

In allied fields a whole variety of activities was under way. Bell towers and cloisters multiplied. Venice began the period of her great mosaic[18] productions. In Germany bronze and enamel work of a high order was developed at Hildesheim and Cologne. Equally famed were the beautiful stained-glass windows in Augsburg, Hildesheim and Tegernsee. During this same period Byzantine art flourished, having entered upon a new golden age which lasted until 1204 when the Crusaders sacked Constantinople.

The great monastic system of Cluny had given the tenth century both the spiritual sources for reform and the physical means—men and their quiet strength which even kings and noblemen respected. But Cluny's power brought about its own decline. In more than two thousand Cluniac monasteries, many of its monks adopted the very things their founders had rejected: soft furs on their robes, luxurious foods, and plenty of them, and servants and manual laborers to do the unpleasant jobs. The monasteries were embellished with costly works of art, gilded statues, mosaics and, worst of all, worship was buried in a maze of processions and unnecessary and endless liturgical innovations which were so onerous that the monks were often drowsy from fatigue.

During the eleventh century a new reform of monastic life was spearheaded by several saintly men, many of whom were in effect exiles from Cluny, for few Cluniacs really wanted a reform of their way of life, though many of them often spoke of the need. The reformers, St. Stephen of Grandmont, St. Bruno, St. Romuald and St. Robert of Molesme, were shunted about from house to house. Each of them, however, was responsible for the initiation of a major new order and every one of them was to have a deep effect upon the medieval church.[19]

St. Bruno founded the order of Carthusian monks at La Grande Chartreuse in Dauphiny in 1084. The mother house, in its solitary valley near Grenoble, to which St. Bruno withdrew, gave its name to the whole order and to each of its monasteries. The Carthusians, whose life is essentially that of hermits, lived under severe rules (total abstinence, perpetual silence, etc.)

and, except on Sundays and during church services, their time was spent by each monk in his cell, i.e., a cottage with provisions for prayer, reading, eating, sleeping, manual work and a tiny garden. Their sleep was broken every night for the three-hour night office; the hair shirt was always worn. This order of monks has never required any reform. The prior of La Grande Chartreuse is general of the order and is the only head of an order who does not reside in Rome. Aside from their rite, which resembles that of the early Christians, the Carthusians devoted their time to manual labor and study. Their houses are traditionally famed for the richness of their libraries. Before the monks were driven from La Grande Chartreuse, five hundred four-pound loaves of bread were distributed weekly as well as other food and winter clothing in large quantities to the poor. A free hospital (one hundred beds) was built and endowed at St. Laurent-du-Pont, and a paper mill was established to provide work for the poor. These works ceased, however, when "the unprofitable servants" of the state were evicted by soldiers of the French Republic, on April 19, 1903. The monastery was returned to the monks in 1941.

There were nine Charterhouses (corruption of the French *Chartreuse*) in England at the time of the Reformation. The last prior of the London Charterhouse was martyred with fifteen of his monks between 1535 and 1540.

Perhaps the most important of the new monastic centers of the time was Citeaux near Dijon, founded by St. Robert of Molesme. An earlier attempt at founding a house at Molesme had seemed successful, but in a dispute his monks drove St. Robert out in 1098 to found another house in the Burgundian swamps of Cistertium or Citeaux (from the French *"cistels"* or "reeds"). With St. Alberic and St. Stephen Harding, St. Robert introduced the strict observance of the Benedictine rule in all its powerful simplicity. Built-in safeguards, such as the General Chapter meetings of all the abbots of monasteries under Citeaux, prevented the gradual relaxation of the rule.

These Cistercian monks, as they were called, were distinguished from other Benedictines by their white habit, white scapular and their admission of lay brothers into the order. They are now divided into two observances: the Common Observance and the More Strict, sometimes erroneously referred to as the Trappists. The abbey of La Trappe, later founded in Canada, adopted a new constitution during the reforms of 1664. Monks following these rules were called "Trappists," but after they were absorbed into the large body of Cistercians of the More Strict Observance in 1892, they were still referred to as "Trappists." The More Strict Observance has perpetual silence (except for necessity), abstinence from flesh, fish and eggs (except for the sick), night office at two A.M., no separate cells, and manual labor for choir monks as well as lay brothers.

Their work was pre-eminently farming, in which they became masters. Throughout Europe, the Cistercians restored farming as a chief occupation of monks. They transformed the wilderness into farmland; swamps were reclaimed by Robert and his monks. Their *Instituta* forbade exploiting serfs; the monks were not allowed to live off parishes or other benefices. They supported themselves by their own labor on their farms, with their herds, flocks, vineyards, forests, quarries and fish-ponds. The English Cistercians were an important factor in the growth of that country's wool culture. The Canadian abbey of La Trappe conducts a government agricultural college. The monks were also dedicated to teaching the ignorant and aiding the poor. The more Strict Observance now has some sixty monasteries with 3,500 monks. Twelve of their houses are in North America.

Citeaux continued nobly for a while, and then began to fail. It might have disappeared altogether had it not been for the great twelfth-century saint, Bernard. In him, as in no other, were personified the Middle Ages and the French spirit in their best characteristics. His writings breathe the richness of his devotion to the wounds of Christ, his deep piety, high ideals and a catholic outlook. Handsome, witty, good-natured, Bernard attracted all who knew him. His youthful ambition to join the Crusades was thwarted by ill health and he was sent instead to study at the college of canons. At twenty-two he became interested in Citeaux and so effective was his enthusiasm on four of his brothers that they, and a number of other relatives—thirty-one in all—followed him into the monastery at Citeaux, where they were welcomed by the great English-born abbot, St. Stephen Harding, who was on the brink of despair since he had not had a vocation in several years.

Three years later Bernard was sent with some monks to found a new house in the lonely forest called the Valley of Wormwood. At first its monks were so poor they had to live on beech leaves. Bernard soon found it possible to provide more regular meals. Eventually the monastery gained a great reputation for holiness. It numbered 130 monks and was parent to many new houses. Its name was changed to Clairvaux, or "illustrious valley."

The Cistercians, to whom St. Bernard brought such vitality, were influential for nearly two centuries, standing as exemplars of monastic life at its finest and purest. By the end of the twelfth century they had 530 abbeys.

One of the chief reasons for their esteem and the rapid spread of the order was St. Bernard. Others were their enthusiastic emphasis on the love of Christ and their cheerful practice of extreme austerities. Lands uncultivated before were showered on them in vast new tracts. Unlike the Cluniacs, who chose the houses by the side of the road, the Cistercians always sought the isolated places to establish their monasteries. Each one had a house for the reception of the poor and an infirmary for the sick.

St. Bernard gained fame in Europe as a scholar, preacher and miracle worker. The Pope enlisted his aid in preaching the Second Crusade in 1145. As a young monk Bernard had often grown weak through vigils and fasting. Though he suffered a severe physical breakdown in 1153, his last act demonstrated his charitable zeal. The Archbishop of Trïer came to Clairvaux seeking Bernard's intervention in a dispute between the people of Metz and the Duke of Lorraine. Bernard made the long trip north and achieved a peaceful settlement by treaty. A short time after he returned to Clairvaux that same year he died on August 21.

Unlike the modern university with its buildings surrounding a campus, or commons, the medieval university was essentially a legal corporation (from the Latin "*universitas*," meaning "corporation") designed to protect its members, guilds of masters and guilds of students, from civil authority. The first real universities arose toward the end of the twelfth century, not out of the cathedral schools established earlier for the training of clerics,[20] but through the voluntary union of teachers and students who shared intellectually a common life. From the ruling princes and the Pope, these *Studia Generalia,* as they were termed, acquired exten-

sive privileges, ecclesiastical benefices as their allotted
foundation and their own peculiar jurisdiction. The first
universities were founded at Paris, Salerno, Bologna
and Oxford; later universities were mostly founded by
temporal princes, but always with the papal privilege.
Oldest of these were at Naples, Toulouse, Rome, Palencia and Salamanca in Spain.

The most outstanding medieval center of higher
learning was the University of Paris, which has always
ranked as the first in Christendom and as the model
for the rest.[21] The prominence gained by the University
of Paris, which began as a guild of masters, was due
to its concentration on theology, the queen of medieval
sciences. Studies in medieval universities were organized into four faculties: theology, law, medicine and
the liberal arts. The medieval university established the
custom of licensed masters, formal examinations and
degrees.

Two names stand out among the pioneers in the
revival of thought: St. Anselm, the Benedictine abbot
of the English monastery, Bec, later the Archbishop of
Canterbury, a champion of Hildebrandine reforming
ideals who supplied scholasticism with an outline and
a goal; and Peter Abelard (1079-1142), one of the
greatest teachers of all times, who came to Paris in
1100, when he was but twenty-one, to study at the
Cathedral School of Notre Dame. After he became
master he established his own school outside the walls
of the city. So great a number of students was attracted
to him through his fame as a dialectician that he is
usually credited with founding the later University of
Paris.

The Parisian phase of his career was interrupted by
the notorious affair with Héloïse, the niece of the canon

of Notre Dame. When their secret relationship was discovered by the canon, he had Abelard physically mutilated. Héloïse was persuaded to become a nun and Abelard himself installed her as abbess of the Convent of the Holy Paraclete. He later retired to a hermitage at Troyes.

In his attempt to bring reason and logic to buttress faith, Abelard "burned his fingers" on the doctrines of atonement and the Holy Trinity. What Saint Bernard complained of as Abelard's rationalistic tendencies led to his condemnation at the Council of Soissons in 1121. Despite this, Abelard continued an active life as a teacher in the hermitage he built. Scholars flocked to learn from him; they provided all his necessities so no household duties distracted him from his studies. It was here, in 1142, that he met death, "the last of the men who were in effect self-contained universities."

Abelard has been hailed as a modern man by those who see in his disputations and queries a challenge to the authority of the Church. Actually Abelard submitted to the decisions of the Church even when it broke his spirit in the closing years of his life. His love of argumentation and his great skill in asking questions and raising doubts about theological and doctrinal issues were his greatest strength. In his book, *Sic et Non* (*Yes and No*) he pointed up some of the Church's teachings requiring explanation. He urged other men to undertake the work of standardization and explanation. In this, he may be said to have begun the work finished over one hundred years later by Thomas Aquinas.

The twelfth and thirteenth centuries indeed constituted a golden age. In no other era could such a movement as the Crusades have taken form. In no other age have reason, philosophy, art, architecture, music and worship reached such a synthesis. Great and noble efforts were made by a number of zealous reformers and churchmen to strengthen the faith of the people. The results were so marked that for many these centuries constituted, above all else, an age of faith.

XV

Heresy and Inquisition

The religious impulse toward Christian poverty and a life of apostolic simplicity which resulted in the tightening of Church discipline, and which found orthodox expression at last in the work of the mendicant friars had, in the preceding twelfth century, at times been perverted into heresy.

Two sects, in particular, were powerful enemies of the Church, and were becoming increasingly dangerous as the twelfth century came to an end. The largest of the two groups were the Waldensians, the "Poor Men of Lyons," originally a sort of order, founded by the well-to-do Lyonese merchant, Peter Waldo, who initiated a reform movement toward evangelical poverty. In a famine in 1176 Waldo gave his money to the poor, came forward as a wandering preacher with companions and called for a return to primitive Christianity. The Waldensians led austere lives and had a reputation for personal sanctity; denouncing wealthy clergy, they insisted upon personal effort and renunciation as more efficacious. They were pacifists and renounced all wars. The "perfect" among the Waldensians made the vows of poverty, chastity and obedience. Laymen celebrated the Eucharist. Anticipating Protestant teachings, they appealed directly to the Gospel, advocating the reading of the Bible by all, and individual interpretation of Scripture.

When their activities became extreme, and some of their members embraced heretical ideas, they were forbidden to preach in public. They continued despite this, and thus incurred excommunication by Pope Lucius III in 1184. The valleys and mountains of northern Italy, near Turin, became a refuge for some of the Waldensians after they were banned.

Ultimately the Waldensians denied the authority of the Church, established themselves as a separate religious body, and attempted to proselytize among Catholics. They taught the priesthood of the laity, as did later Protestant sects—that is, every just man could absolve, consecrate and preach the Gospel without sacramental ordination. Throughout the Middle Ages, their efforts led to the burnings and massacres of their members. In the sixteenth century they established contact with the Reformation, and continued their religious war with the Italian State, which, of course, never fell prey to Reformation heresies. They did not receive political and religious freedom until 1848.

The more dangerous, more widespread sect—the Albigensians—were a group from the city of Albi, their stronghold in southern France. Here they were heavily concentrated but the sect was to be found also in northern Italy, throughout the Mediterranean area and in Bulgaria, the apparent source of the heresy. Technically they were not Christians at all, but Provençal inheritors of the dualistic system of Manichaeism. They also are called the Cathari, or "the pure," as the Novatians of the third century had termed themselves. However, the Albigensians did not spring from them. This heretical sect rejected any visible church, every spiritual and secular authority, war, and the death penalty. Dualism lay at the root of their teaching—the division of creation into the good things of the spirit and the essentially evil things of the flesh or matter. They had only one sacrament, "the Baptism of the Spirit" or *Consolamentum*, which, however, only the "perfect" among them received, that is, those who strove to fulfill rigidly all their extreme ascetic practices (renunciation of all material, physical and sexual contacts). The rest, or "the believers," who merely promised to fulfill these ascetic practices at some future date, received the *Consolamentum* only on their death-bed.

Though St. Bernard and the Cistercians preached against them, the sect continued to grow in strength. They seized Church property by force, drove bishops and the Catholic clergy from their sees and churches, and by the beginning of the thirteenth century presented a serious danger to both Church and state. The sect condemned private property, opposed marriage and family life, advocated suicide, murder and the destruction of churches and monasteries. These facts make it easier to understand the extreme measures taken by both the Church and state against them.

In 1178 the Count of Toulouse, Raymond VI, along with the Kings of France and England requested Pope Alexander III to send a legate with full powers to repress the heresy. This was done, but only a few retracted. Then an unexpected tragedy brought events to a bloody conclusion. Pope Innocent III, in his zeal to convert the Albigensians and bring peace, finally excommunicated the uncooperative Raymond VI, through his papal legate, a Cistercian monk. Within the year, one of Raymond's attendants rushed upon the monk and killed him. This outrage came at a time when Pope Innocent was employing only peaceful methods. The Pontiff then decided to summon the French king to a crusade against the Albigensians.

This precipitated a real war, which was conducted with great cruelty on both sides.[22] Under Simon de Montfort the crusaders devastated Languedoc but resultant political squabbles limited the religious effectiveness of this crusade.[23]

The war against the Albigensians raged for nearly twenty years. Launched by the Pope as a purely religious movement, it gradually deteriorated into civil strife for possession of the lands of Toulouse, which were finally taken by the King of France in 1229. The war ended, but heresy still remained strong throughout parts of southern France where the Albigensians carried on their activities in secret. The ecclesiastical authorities decided that these conditions called for a judicial method to combat heresy. Gregory IX (1227-41) thereupon originated the papal Inquisition in 1233.

The Inquisition, not to be confused with the Spanish Inquisition of a later date, was a new tribunal, its judicial machinery set up by and responsible to the Papacy. Its business was to discover and punish heretics. The Franciscans and more especially the Dominicans were generally employed by the Pope for this work. A new body of law and criminal practice gradually gathered around this institution; it was influenced by the contemporary revival of Roman law in two important respects: in the introduction of death as the penalty for a convicted heretic and in the use of torture in examining the accused.[24] In reality, civil laws in Western Europe were far more severe than Church laws against heretics until the Popes sanctioned the use of the stake and torture.

According to the machinery set up by Gregory IX and elaborated by Innocent IV and later Popes, the papal inquisitors traveled around to the towns under suspicion (in much the same way the new assize jus-

tices traveled around England), and called on all heretics to appear before them, or called on people who
knew of heretics to denounce them secretly.[25] Once
accused, a person found it almost impossible to prove
his innocence, but if he admitted error and accepted
penance, he suffered no harm. Those who denied they
were heretics could be tortured until they confessed.
Admitted heretics who refused to recant could be
tortured to persuade them to change their opinions.
Theoretically torture could be employed only once,
and never to the extent of inflicting serious injury, but
there were instances where torture was often "extended." [26] The most obstinate heretics and those who
later retracted their confessions were handed over to
the civil authorities for punishment, and this usually
meant burning at the stake.

Even though we bear in mind that the Inquisition
was an instrument employed by the Pope to defend
civilization against the most pernicious dangers in a
time of crisis, and even though we recognize that the
procedure and methods employed were not at odds
with the standards of an admittedly intolerant and
religiously homogeneous age, the Inquisition "is totally
repugnant to modern standards of just legal procedures
and toleration." The inquisitorial method went against
the earlier Christian tradition which disassociated the
use of violence from religious procedures. No Catholic
historian attempts any longer to defend it. Its major
defects were the lack of protection for the innocent
and the difficulty of preventing abuses by overzealous
inquisitors like Robert le Bougre. In all fairness it
must be stated that abuses were on the whole com-
paratively rare, and the numbers receiving the death
penalty have been grossly exaggerated. Two careful
church historians have concluded that the Inquisition

was, in short, "a case of churchmen failing to rise above the barbarities of their environment." [27] As the Jesuit, Father James Broderick, has said, it was "a horrible and hateful thing, a grave backsliding, not of the Church, but of churchmen, which no Catholic ought now to lift a finger to defend, except from exaggeration or the too obvious efforts . . . to turn it to controversial advantage." [28]

XVI

The Great Mendicant Orders

The thirteenth century was marked by an unprecedented religious ardor, revealed through remarkable spiritual undertakings, such as the crusading movement, the building of cathedrals, the synthesis of faith and reason in scholastic philosophy, and in the new religious orders which came into existence one after another.

The century also saw rapid and profound changes in medieval society. The Papacy expanded in the temporal sphere (although running through the century was the age-old conflict between the spiritual and temporal arms of society). The feudal lord had meanwhile attained the height of his power and in continental Europe held many of the rights of sovereignty. There was a renascence under way in the arts and sciences. Important shifts took place in the economic sphere, under the newly found order of the king's peace: the development of banking, the growth of cities, and the organization of guilds with their patron saints and chaplains who observed the numerous religious feasts that filled the Church calendar. People dwelled near the castles or the great monastic establishments or in the thriving medieval towns and hamlets; here the faithful attended Mass and, less frequently (about once a year), received Holy Communion. Since heretics were widespread, since both the laity and clergy were not educated sufficiently in theological and moral truths, and since up to that time preaching was the special concern of bishops, an order of preachers was badly needed. The new social structure called for religious ministrations different from those given to country folk.

In a setting such as this the great mendicant orders were born. Like many other outstanding religious figures of his exciting age, St. Dominic (1170-1221) was born of noble parents at Calaruega in old Castile. He was educated in the public schools of Palencia, which were soon joined with Salamanca. In his native Castile, Dominic had tried vainly to sell himself into slavery in order to ransom captives held by the Moors. At twenty-eight he was received into the Institute of Canons Regular of St. Augustine, and soon after accompanied his bishop to Rome to seek permission to do missionary work among the Tartars. Instead, Innocent III sent Dominic on a diplomatic mission in 1205 which accidentally brought him into contact with the Cistercian mission to the Albigenses. As Dominic went about his apostolic work, he soon realized that the official pomp of the papal legates was a great hindrance to the work of reconversion. A clergy detached from wealth and material comfort, as the ascetics of some heretical sects were, was needed, as was the ability to defend the Faith against current false doctrines. Only in this way, Dominic thought, could the wavering or the lapsed Catholic be won back to Christ.

He then gathered around him a body of preachers, who wandered about Languedoc preaching to the Albigenses when they could. In their lives, all St. Dominic's ideals, including a rule of absolute poverty, found a place. It was during his sojourn among the

Albigenses that St. Dominic instituted the devotion of the Rosary, by which he obtained marvelous results.

From these chance beginnings there grew a religious order of a new kind altogether. The Friars-Preachers were not monks confined to a monastery, or linked together in a collection of houses, but they were an army of priests organized under a Master-General in provinces, ready to go wherever they were needed. At the Fourth Lateran Council (1215) they were placed directly under the authority of the Pope. As it happened, the Dominicans were the first Catholic missionaries to achieve any success in reconverting the Albigenses.

As Dominic intensified his efforts, his followers multiplied. In 1216, they numbered sixteen, and had received the gift of a house and a church in Toulouse for their work. Pope Honorius III (1216-27) approved the plan for the new order, which adopted the rule of St. Augustine, and the novel vocation of study, preaching and teaching. Before the close of the century, the Dominicans had already attained the character of a society of professional theologians and highly effective orators. Working closely with the newly founded Friars Minor, the Order of Preachers spread all over Europe, attracting to their ranks some of the most brilliant intellects of the time, and founding houses in every Christian country.

For all its rapidity, the expansion of the Dominicans was not nearly so rapid as that of the other contemporary new order—the Friars Minor. Italy gave many great names and many revered saints to the world, but none has been more a saint or has had more power to make the world see the beauty in holiness than St. Francis of Assisi (1181-1226). This extraordinary personality, with his quiet simplicity, engaging wit, talent for music and unqualified dedication to humanity, has captured the imagination of millions, Catholic and Protestant alike. Some of the things that go to make up the strange and complicated beauty of the Franciscan story are his absolute devotion to poverty and the love he had for all God's creatures in the ranks inferior to man. To this day the Franciscan monastery abounds in flowers and gardens, and doves have a special place here because of St. Francis' protection of them. Another of his characteristics was the association of religion with gaiety rather than grimness.

The story of the conversion of this John Bernadoni (called Francis, or the Frenchman, because of his early attraction to French fashions and the French way of life) is one which belongs especially to the thirteenth century but it later became the heritage of all the centuries. On his way to participate in one of the endless struggles that ravaged Italy, Francis came upon a poverty-stricken gentleman, and gave him his own magnificent armor and clothing. In visions which followed, Francis was urged "to serve the master." Gradually he began to meditate on the Gospel. While riding one day near Assisi he met a leper covered with running sores. The young nobleman dismounted, and as the leper reached for alms, Francis kissed his hand. From that time on, self-renunciation and devotion to the poor and sick became his lifework.

A deeper conversion came later, and he began preaching the Gospel, living by its word, barefooted and in utter poverty. With a handful of friends, living in huts built of twigs and hay, he preached repentance "with a tongue of fire," and he taught of the true happiness that came from following Our Lord's example. For a living, his followers depended on what the charity of the town gave them. There had been earlier lay movements to live a life of consecrated poverty and to preach that life to others, but Francis found a radically new approach to Christ and drew followers by the hundreds. In 1208 he went to Rome and sought the blessing of Pope Innocent III on this new way of life.

After receiving the Pope's approval for the new order of Friars Minor, Francis continued to preach with astounding success, traveling as far east as the Holy Land. Mainly, he and his followers devoted themselves to preaching in the towns. As Bernard loved the valleys, and Benedict the mountains, and Dominic the famous cities, Francis loved the towns and preached in the vernacular to ordinary men and women in rural and urban settlements. His movement was not designed for those who were won over to heresy or were wavering in their faith; his was a mission to Catholics whose lives were disordered morally, in whom worldliness and material wealth had dried up the springs of charity. The long struggle between Pope and emperor provides us with opportunity enough to examine evidence that the morals of Christendom, in high places as well as low, were far from the state of perfection that was the goal of St. Francis.

Soon however, Francis was called back to cope with dissension within his order. At a great assembly near Assisi he resigned from active leadership, with the conviction that his followers had become too unwieldy for him to manage.[29] In 1224, on Monte La Verna near Arezzo, where he had withdrawn into solitude, St. Francis received the stigmata, the impression on his hands, side and feet of the five bleeding wounds of Christ. In 1226 he died and two years later he was canonized a saint.

His original rules of austerity and poverty were

later mitigated, and out of his ideals came groups of varying strictness: the Friars Minor, the Friars Minor Conventual, and the Friars Minor Capuchin. Like St. Dominic, St. Francis developed three orders, one for men, one for women and the order of lay brethren. One of his followers was St. Clare (1193-1253), who founded the austere order of women known as "the poor Clares" based on the ideals of St. Francis. Her first little convent was at San Damiano, at the base of a hill on the outskirts of Assisi. St. Francis gave it to her when he left for the Porziuncola. The beautiful church of St. Clare, raised as a monument over her tomb in Assisi, is a typical Gothic church of the thirteenth century, very dim and dark, but there is no church where the stained-glass windows are so bright and gem-like. "It seems suggestive of the soul shutting itself off in the cloister from human sight and sounds so that it may gaze through apertures upon the heavenly light."[30]

The establishment of the Third Order of St. Francis, the tertiaries or lay brethren, a real religious order open to lay folk living in the world and following their own vocations, was one special reason for the great Franciscan success story. These men and women placed themselves under the direction of the Friars and a modified version of the Friar's own rule. Chiefly through these so-called Third Orders for the laity did the Mendicants perform their pastoral work. With these groups begins the history of confraternities within the Church, without which even today we could not imagine a successful care of souls. The Third Orders were for the laity a school of sanctity. Today the lay tertiaries number more than one million.[31]

Among the earliest Franciscan Tertiaries were Saint Louis of France and Saint Elizabeth of Thuringia. The former we met undertaking the last Crusade. The latter, born in 1207, was the daughter of Andrew II, King of Hungary. Betrothed at an early age to Louis IV, Landgrave of Thuringia, Elizabeth was as devoted to the poor of her kingdom as Louis was devoted to her. (Unlike many such medieval arrangements, theirs turned out to be a marriage of love.) In her zeal she practically emptied the royal coffers, conveying apronloads of bread personally to the poor.

Louis, called on the Crusades, died at the age of twenty-seven en route to the Holy Land. Having vowed never to remarry should he fail to return, Elizabeth, already leading a life of deprivation, penance and prayer, joined the Third Order of St. Francis. Forced to leave the great castle where she had reigned as queen, she established a hospital for the poor at Marburg, where she worked at menial tasks and nursed the sick. At the early age of twenty-four, she died and was four years later declared a saint. When her incorruptible body was transferred to the church erected in her honor, the Emperor Frederick II, the most powerful ruler in Europe, came to place his own crown upon her head.

Sharing the company of St. Francis in popular devotion is his disciple, St. Anthony of Padua. Anthony is called "of Padua" although he was really born in Portugal because he did so much for the people of Padua where he ended his life and where his relics lie. Here another beautiful Gothic church is the monument which houses the tomb of the saint. Most beautiful of all the churches in this area, however, is the Church of St. Francis in Assisi, whose walls bear the story of the saint's life in paintings.

The Preachers and Friars Minor were the principal, but by no means the only, orders of friars. There were

also the Carmelites, whose history began in 1155 when
a hermitage of Western men was founded on Mount
Carmel in Palestine by St. Berthold. The hermits
spread to Europe from Cyprus, and under the English
St. Simon Stock they modified their rule and became
mendicant friars. The reforms of the sixteenth century
resulted in the formation of two independent branches
of the Carmelite order, the Shod Carmelites of the
Strict Observance, and the Discalced (Barefooted)
Carmelites, who occupy the Mother House on Mount
Carmel. The change from a congregation of hermits
to the Mendicants was made by still another order with
a great future, the Augustinian Hermits, which came
into being between 1243 and 1256, and which, like
the Dominicans with whom it had in common the rule
of St. Augustine, zealously devoted itself to study.
Toward the end of the fifteenth century this order had
the remarkable membership of thirty thousand. It was
the Order of Augustinian hermits, to which Martin
Luther belonged and it was hard hit, as is well known,
by the Reformation.

What was essentially new about the orders of Mendicants was not the individual poverty of their members. The new element was that even the monastery
was not permitted to possess anything. The Mendicants'
monastery was not an abbey with forests, fish ponds,
arable land, tenants and dependent peasants, like the
Cistercian abbeys of an earlier time, but offered a
minimum of accommodations such as a man required
for an austere life—a few rooms near a church, perhaps a small garden, and nothing else. For the Mendicant, home was no longer the monastery but the society of the order. Stability and permanent location,
the basis of monastic life since Benedict, was abandoned. Thus a type of order was created which met

the challenge of the growing social change. The Mendicants lived among the people, exercising the care of souls. The people did not have to go to them; they went to the people. The Mendicants went to the rural folk, the children, the soldiers, into prisons, among heretics and pagans. With them begins an entirely new epoch in the care of souls.

XVII

Scholasticism

A survey of the highlights in medieval culture and learning such as this must neglect the various periods of cultural revival during the Carolingian Renaissance, the Ottonian Renaissance and the twelfth-century Renaissance. But we have seen from our brief account that in many abbeys throughout Western Europe the early Church Fathers and classical writings of ancient times were studied. One of the great accomplishments of the medieval monasteries was the preservation of the Latin and Greek classics.

Neither does space permit adequate attention to the refined expressions of piety that appeared, as never before or since in Church history, in the devotional theology associated with names like Bernard of Clairvaux, Hugo and Richard of St. Victor, St. Gertrude or St. Francis of Assisi, who personifies a degree of closeness to God and union with Him such as has been attained by very few others.

The universities were almost solely responsible for the new learning of the Middle Ages. Including the transient ones, over eighty new medieval universities were founded before 1300. These were the forums for the great philosophico-theological controversies of the day, out of which would come a transformation resulting in new methods of explaining and defending the Faith. Already during St. Dominic's own lifetime, the

Dominicans began to lecture in 1218, at the University of Paris, where, with Albert the Great and Thomas Aquinas, they attained the height of their fame. Thus, by the thirteenth century the medieval universities were firmly established, and the newly founded Mendicant orders, dedicated to study and learning, came to them. The elements were now present for the great flowering of mystical and theological speculation of the High Middle Ages which has never been surpassed. It remains then for us to follow briefly the progress of medieval thought which would synthesize philosophy and theology in the service of the Church.

A new kind of scholar, "the Schoolman," came into being, who brought the clear light of intellect to bear on the problems of God, man and the universe in a way that had never been done before. Scholasticism, the result, was not a sudden, consciously planned movement. From earliest times Christian scholars had been anxious to show that there was *no* contradiction between true science and the one True Faith. They wanted to develop a mode of thought which would demonstrate this. In other words, they wished to reconcile human reason with divine revelation, or philosophy with theology. Scholasticism, the work of the Schoolmen of the thirteenth century, was the medieval attempt to systematize and explain revealed truth in correlation with a philosophical system. The truths of the Catholic Church supplied the field for organized and systematic thought. Aristotle, accepted by thousands as the world's leading philosopher, supplied the method of reasoning, the cold, hard method of logic. In adapting Aristotle's method to their purpose, the Scholastics brought reasoning to its highest perfection in a system which climaxed the Middle Ages and helped form modern Europe. They accomplished a twofold purpose: first, philosophy and theology were placed in their separate domains but not separated entirely, and second, the use of reason was advocated without denying the validity of divine revelation.

The first step in the intellectual revival in the medieval universities was the gradual discovery of the whole body of Aristotle's teaching—a discovery that was more or less completed by the first quarter of the thirteenth century.[32] It is interesting to note that this Aristotelian body of learning, science, logic and philosophy was introduced into the West by Arabs, Moors and Jews. Christian scholars were familiar not only with the Latin translations of Aristotle but also with those two great scholars of Córdoba, the Arab Averroës, and the Jew, Maimonides. From the Greeks, as well as from the Arabs and Jews, flowed new currents into the stream of Christian philosophy. It is difficult for us to realize the impact, on the two generations that first saw it, of the gradual unfolding of all that Aristotle's genius had accomplished by the time of his death in 322 B.C., for this great Greek philosopher possessed one of the few really encyclopedic minds ever produced by the West. In his writings we find wide and detailed observation of life.[33]

Philosophical and theological questions began to be debated passionately everywhere; theologians and philosophers fought each other and argued with great fury. But especially were they debated at the University of Paris, the first and most famous of all universities, from about the time of its foundation in 1205. By the reign of Gregory IX (1227-41) the Popes were making the study of Aristotle's *Physics* and *Metaphysics* obligatory for all clerical candidates for a degree. Aristotelianism had gradually become what it still remains, "the most precious of all the Catholic Church's human aids in the explanation and rational defense of Revelation."[34]

In tracing the origins of Scholasticism beyond Aristotle, it would be possible to begin with Augustine and his admonition: "Understand so that you may believe— believe so that you may understand." Boethius (d. 524), "an oasis in a barren stretch of history," extolled the consolations of philosophy and translated Aristotle along with other Greeks.[35]

These represent only halting steps. Real continuity in the line of Schoolmen begins with John Scotus Erigena (815-77). A lonely scholar and a faithful son of the Church, he mastered Greek and Latin, revived philosophical thought and tried to fuse neo-Platonism with Christianity. Holy Scripture was used as his source of reference. For him, true religion and true philosophy were identical; both rested on the unity of God. Faith, he believed, has limits. It is "a certain beginning by which knowledge of the creator begins to be produced in the rational nature." Faith and reason could never appear in opposition to each other. Although he never claimed that he was an independent thinker, Erigena regarded Church doctrine as dynamic and therefore attempted an original approach to religion and philosophy. This led him to theological positions which now often appear to approach pantheism, and for which he narrowly escaped persecution. While his influence may have been greater with the mystics than with the logicians of the later Middle Ages, Erigena is a watershed figure: Scholasticism would flow from him, but he also stood at the end of an age. His work "synthesizes the philosophical accomplishments of fifteen centuries, and appears as the final achievement of ancient philosophy."[36]

A stormy period of controversy followed during

which dialectic (the method of the "yes" and "no" in confrontation as a way toward truth) emerged as a new tool for the Schoolmen, and Scholasticism was equipped to serve the Orthodox cause.

St. Anselm (1033-1109) was of even greater importance than Erigena as a Christian philosopher. Father Hertling calls him the real founder of Scholasticism. Though he was not a Scholastic, that school of thought embodied many of his concepts. This "second Augustine" and "precursor of Aquinas" was the thinker who provided Scholasticism with an outline and a goal.[37] The ascetic existence maintained by this Benedictine Abbot of Bec in Normandy and later Archbishop of Canterbury (1109) was frequently interrupted by political activity. His philosophy was largely a justification of Church practices and dogma. He was convinced that the comprehension of divine truth was the result of faith, not reason. "I do not seek to understand that I may believe, but I believe in order to understand. For this also I believe, that unless I believed, I should not understand." In his most famous book, *Cur Deus Homo* (*Why Did God Become Man*), Anselm tried to answer questions concerning the doctrine of man's redemption. In his *Proslogion* he offered the classic ontological argument for the existence of God—by showing the inconceivability of God's nonexistence.

Peter Abelard, who was an antagonist of St. Anselm, showed his ability to reach the roots of philosophical problems. As we have seen, his *Sic et Non* constituted an early dialectic. In his philosophical speculations, Abelard anticipated the difficulties certain Scholastics were to have in their application of the canons of reason to the apostolic tradition.[38]

To this age of early Scholasticism—as the period

before the rise of universities is called—belongs Peter of Novare, known as Peter Lombard (d. 1164), who proved himself a true servant of the Church in his preparation of the *Sentences,* the classic theological text on which the later scholastics, including St. Thomas Aquinas, commented.

As Father Hertling writes, the thirteenth century can be compared in the wealth of its theological production and intellectual attainment only with the period around 400 which produced the great Church Fathers. Seldom has Christianity found intellects so useful to ecclesiastical purposes as did the medieval Church in those three great saints: Albertus Magnus, Thomas Aquinas and St. Bonaventura. The first two were Dominicans, the last was a Friar Minor. The greatest of the three was, of course, St. Thomas Aquinas, whose synthesis of revealed and rational truth represents the climax of theological effort, a medieval achievement as monumental and impressive as the cathedrals.

St. Albert the Great, or Albertus Magnus (1193-1280), born at Lauingen-on-the-Danube in Swabian Germany, and educated in Padua and Bologna, is considered to be the first representative of humanism during the Middle Ages. He is often referred to as "Doctor Universalis" or the "Catholic Aristotle," the complete scientist and the complete theologian, who, in Aristotle's spirit, "set himself to acquire and make accessible to others all that could be known of the created universe and its relation to its Creator."[39]

After entering the Dominican Order in 1223, Albertus Magnus gained a reputation as a professor of theology, known throughout Europe. He taught at Hildesheim, Ratisbon, Strasbourg and later Cologne. In 1245 he went to the University of Paris, where he publicly expounded the doctrines of Aristotle—accept-

ing whatever parts of it he found true. It was at Paris that
Albertus Magnus became the teacher of St. Thomas
Aquinas, introducing him to Aristotle, thus training the
greatest of all Catholic thinkers. Thomas was bur-
lesqued by his fellow students as "the dumb ox of
Sicily," but St. Albert prophesied that "this dumb ox
will fill the world with his bellowing." St. Thomas contributed greatly to the future history of all European
thought by the use he made of St. Albert's scientifically
drawn distinction between philosophy and theology.
Albert believed in the defense of knowledge for its
intrinsic value, and that philosophy was an integral
part of that knowledge. He was more the compiler than
the systematic thinker and more the commentator than
creator of constructive philosophies.

St. Albert taught at Cologne from 1248 to 1254,
was twice provincial of his order, and was later named
Bishop of Ratisbon, or Regensburg. He remained the
devoted friend of his famous pupil, St. Thomas, until
his death in 1274. One of Albertus' last works was
written in his pupil's defense. He died in Cologne in
1280.

John of Fidanza (1221-74), surnamed Fra Bonaventura after he entered the Order of Franciscans in
1240, studied in Paris but was excluded from the
University in 1255 because he supported Thomas
Aquinas in a dispute. Though readmitted in 1257, he
was again taken away from the life of the universities
at the age of thirty-six, to become general of his order.
Philosopher, mystic and dogmatic theologian, his central theme was the study of God. Man, he thought,
possesses an imperfect but very certain knowledge of
the Supreme Being. St. Bonaventura represents the
Augustinian tradition within the Church.

In St. Thomas Aquinas (1225-74) Aristotle at last

met the Catholic perfectly equipped to understand him, to distinguish him from the commentators, and to show that his thought was in harmony with Catholic doctrine. All non-Catholic philosophers and historians regard the theological doctrines promulgated by Aquinas as reaching the very summit of that extraordinary intellectual activity climaxed in thirteenth-century Scholasticism.

Thomas was born around 1225 in the medieval fortress of Roccasecca in Naples, near the little town of Aquino to which he owed his surname. His father was the Count of Aquino, a nephew of the Emperor Frederick Barbarossa, and on his mother's side he was descended from the Norman barons who had conquered Sicily two centuries before. The Aquino family could also claim relationship to St. Gregory the Great, St. Louis of France and St. Ferdinand of Castile. God's watchful providence over this child was strikingly manifested when a terrible thunderstorm burst over the castle, and his nurse and little sister were struck dead in the same room where Thomas slept on, unharmed. Hence the popular devotion to St. Thomas as patron against thunderstorms.

When he was only five years old, his education was begun by the monks of the nearby monastery, Monte Cassino. From there he was sent with his tutor to the University of Naples, where he studied six years. When he was seventeen, Thomas entered the Dominican monastery at Naples, much against the wishes of his family, shocked by the idea of a nobleman becoming a begging friar. The Countess Theodora, Thomas' mother, was determined that he should never be a Dominican; and his father, who would gladly have seen him take the Benedictine habit hoping that, like one of his uncles, he would rise to the dignity of Abbot of Monte Cassino and thus help to enrich the impoverished family, despised the Mendicant Order. Thomas was asked to accompany the General of his order from Rome to Paris, to avoid encounters with his irate parents. The Countess, meanwhile, sent orders to her two elder sons, then serving in the emperor's army in Italy, to waylay their brother and bring him back to the family castle, where he was shut up in the tower for almost a year "until he should regain his senses." But in the end his firmness prevailed, and he was allowed to return to the order. This was the most outwardly dramatic event of his life; henceforth all his energies were directed to teaching, explaining and defending the Catholic Faith.

The General of his order again selected Thomas to accompany him to Cologne, where he became a student of the renowned Dominican professor, Albertus Magnus. Between 1245 and 1246 Thomas accompanied Albertus Magnus on a visit to the University of Paris, where Thomas became involved in the dispute between the university and the Dominican Friars as to the liberty of teaching. Thomas advocated with great energy the rights claimed by the Friars.

In 1257, St. Thomas received a doctor's degree from the Sorbonne, where he soon gained great distinction as lecturer in theology. A few years later we find him lecturing in London, Rome, Bologna and elsewhere. The Pope offered to make him Abbot of Monte Cassino (to please his parents) or Archbishop of Naples, but Thomas refused both.

As Martin Marty says, it is not possible to do justice to a thinker like Aquinas by brief reference to his thought. But that writer has at least placed it in its proper context. Aquinas' most important work, which he modestly declared was written for beginners, is that great edifice of medieval Christian thought, the *Summa Theologica,* still the official text in Catholic schools and colleges and the core of all Catholic philosophical studies.

Thomas insisted on the rights of philosophy as an independent science. Reason and faith are distinct. Reason is supreme in its own domain, but he removed many areas of thought from its realm. There are things that reason cannot discover; yet these mysteries, unattainable by reason, are neither irrational nor beyond rational explanation. Such areas for example, as the Incarnation (God taking human form), the Resurrection or the Trinity, are vastly different from the rationally accessible ones: the existence of God and many of His attributes. Neither Albertus Magnus nor Aquinas was a slavish follower of Aristotle: both differed from him on important points but they accepted the main lines of Aristotle's realism, and showed that Christian doctrine could be expressed in terms of it.

Aquinas' thought moved along two lines, the philosophical and the theological, where he devoted himself to a discussion of the sacraments and Biblical exegesis. The Holy Eucharist was the great sacrament among the seven Christ instituted. Thomas wrote the beautiful devotional hymn "*Adoro te devote,*" along with the celebrated stanzas of "*Pange Lingua*" and "*Panis Angelicus,*" all in honor of the Blessed Sacrament. As thinker, hymnist, devotionist and disputant, he towers over all his contemporaries, indeed over all churchmen.

St. Thomas died in 1274 on his way to Lyons to attend a general council for the purpose of uniting the Greek and Latin Churches. Of his death, his biographer wrote that he was "rather ravished to heaven by the force of his greater love than by that of his illness." [40] The title "Doctor of the Church," was granted to him by Pope Pius V in 1567.[41]

To his contemporaries, the synthesis contained in St. Thomas' *Summa* was a revolutionary thing. Many of his leading theses fell short of the traditional methods of apologetics, and came into direct conflict with the school of thought led by St. Bonaventura, following the works of Plato and St. Augustine. For a long time after his death the followers of St. Thomas fought for his ideas, which were being undermined by critics within Catholic ranks. Among them were two keen Franciscan logicians, John Duns Scotus and William of Ockham.

John Duns Scotus (1265-1308) criticized both Augustine and Aquinas and attempted to destroy their notions of matter, form and potency. William of Ockham (1300-1349) denied the possibility of proving God's existence or uncovering his attributes by reason. No other Christian thinker of the Middle Ages, not even Abelard, rejected so many or such important assumptions prevalent in his times as did Ockham.

Pioneers of thought rarely live to see their ideas triumph, and St. Thomas was no exception to this rule. Though Rome never condemned him, the theologians of Paris did more than once, and so, too, did the prelates of his own order. Not until fifty years after his death was his position established as entirely orthodox. Father Hughes calls this slowness to recognize the genius of Thomas Aquinas "one of the major tragedies of medieval Catholicism." Aquinas was canonized a saint by Pope John XXII in 1323, and his authority as a theologian was officially established in the encyclical *Aeterni Patris* (1879) by Pope Leo XIII, who made him the patron of all Catholic schools.

Although medieval Scholasticism, to which this great

saint contributed so much, by no means solved all questions and left a great deal for later theologians to do, yet the enrichment through Scholasticism of religious life within the Church was extraordinarily great. It gave to Catholic piety a new impulse which was of the utmost importance.

If St. Thomas brought medieval theology to the summit of perfection, the great Italian poet of the Middle Ages, Dante Alighieri (1265-1321), found the true and final synthesis of medieval thought and culture which he wove into his great Christian poem, *The Divine Comedy*. Dante lived a full life as poet, philosopher, statesman and soldier. He prepared himself for his great work as a lyric poet by studying the writings of Dominican and Franciscan philosophers. He was most impressed by the Scholasticism of St. Thomas Aquinas, whose influence can be seen in the stanzas in which St. Thomas is chosen to relate the life of St. Francis. Dante chose St. Bonaventura to tell the story of St. Dominic.

The Divine Comedy is the most grandiose and cosmic creation in world literature. The beauty of the whole depends on its grand plan, whose vast sweep reminds us of the plan of Plato's *Republic*, or of a Gothic cathedral, or of the great theological *Summa*. Tieck speaks of the great poem as "the voice of ten silent centuries." With Aquinas and Dante, the medieval synthesis was complete.[42]

XVIII

Empire versus Papacy

The renewed struggle between the Church and Caesar did not begin as a fight to wrest from the emperor rights he had usurped over the Church's life, but as a defense of the Church's newly won freedom from an attempt to impose by force something of the Caesaropapism, as practiced formerly in the East, under which the Church there had withered.

After the Concordat of Worms in 1122, there followed a short interlude during which the power of the Papacy grew more solid under the guiding force of men like St. Bernard. However, Italian factions again confronted each other, seized power in Rome, and under their domination the Papacy almost experienced a relapse into the dark days of the tenth century.

In 1152 the German Emperor, Conrad, died and the rivalry of the two Houses (Guelphs and Ghibellines) was for the time adjusted by the election of his nephew, Frederick of Swabia (1152-90), called Barbarossa (his mother was a Guelph). No other king pacified the perpetual German unrest as he did in the first two years after his accession. Pope Eugene III (1145-54) made a treaty with the young Hohenstaufen ruler in which Frederick I agreed to aid the Papacy against the hostile Romans and Normans in return for the imperial crown. This presented an opportunity for the German Emperor to step forward once again as protector of the Church—an arrangement which would have brought advantages to both parties. Instead there arose a protracted conflict between Emperor and Pope which lasted for almost a century, which weakened the empire, severely altered European politics, and damaged the prestige of the Papacy.

The struggle did not involve religious beliefs. Opponents of the Pope generally acknowledged the spiritual authority of the Church. They even conceded that religion formed the basis for civil authority. But Frederick was not content to be German king. Intense ambition urged him to the restoration of the imperial ideal. The Hohenstaufen dynasty devoted all its efforts to becoming territorial overlord of Italy. In their attempts to control Italy the emperors found it necessary to undermine the temporal authority of Popes. Originally the Papacy had no intention of weakening the German emperors and the Empire. On the contrary, the Papacy needed and wanted protection. It so happened that almost all the Popes with whom the Hohenstaufen had to deal were extremely competent men. They quickly perceived that the Hohenstaufen no longer really wanted to be protectors of the Church. Modern rulers in the true sense, they embraced the more profane idea of the state. They wished to destroy clerical independence and to set up a territorial empire in which the Popes would occupy the subordinate position of first imperial bishop, or something of that nature. These Popes were simply unwilling to be subordinate. Therefore the emperors proceeded systematically to invade Italy, "depose" recalcitrant Popes, and support anti-Popes who were often the emperors' personal choice. In turn, the Papacy exercised the right to excommunicate and depose rulers who thus interfered with the freedom and unity of the Church.

In keeping with the terms of his treaty, Barbarossa went to Italy in 1155, put an end to the Roman Republic there, and received the imperial crown from the hands of Adrian IV (1154-59), the only English Pope who ever sat on St. Peter's throne, and as it turned out, a man who was determined to uphold every claim that Pope St. Gregory VII himself had ventured to make. Even at this first meeting with the Roman Pontiff, Barbarossa at the outset refused to hold the Pope's stirrup in welcoming him—until his aides finally convinced Frederick that it was a traditional ceremony which implied no humiliation.

Though Frederick may have had other plans, he was forced to return hastily to Germany where unrest had erupted once again. Adrian was left to work out a policy of his own—which he did with remarkable success. In 1158 Barbarossa returned to Italy mainly to enforce submission on Milan, which had formed the Lombard League to resist encroachments on the autonomy of Italian cities. Milan was destroyed by his troops and Frederick exacted feudal oaths from the Italian bishops. He also issued a series of decrees Caesaropapist in tone. Pope Adrian IV, now shielded by his alliance with King William of Sicily, was preparing to excommunicate Frederick when he died suddenly at Anagni in 1159.

A disputed papal election followed in which Alexander III (1159-81) received the vote of a majority of cardinals. Alexander, who had been professor of canon law at the University of Bologna, was destined to become one of the greatest of Popes. None other than Voltaire himself claimed he did more for human rights than any man in the Middle Ages. He promoted the intellectual movement then under way, and by a combination of firmness and diplomacy he secured recognition of rights for which the saint, Thomas Becket, died. The Emperor contested the election of Alexander and a minority of cardinals selected Victor IV, whom Barbarossa quickly recognized. The kings of England and France, many German bishops, the entire Cistercian order, and the renascent Lombard League supported the claims of Alexander III, undoubtedly the strongest. In 1166, Barbarossa with his great army swept irresistibly down on Rome. The Pope, after having excommunicated the Emperor, fled to the Normans in the South. When Victor IV died, Barbarossa set up a new anti-Pope, Paschal III, came into Rome and had himself again crowned emperor in 1167. His army, encamped outside Rome, was then practically decimated by pestilence. The Emperor led the few straggling survivors back to Germany. Not until 1174 did he return with a new army to Italy. After a vain attempt to besiege the Lombard fortress, Alessandria, his army was decisively defeated by the troops of the Lombard League at Legnano in 1176. Concluding an armistice, Frederick Barbarossa first made peace with Pope Alexander III, whom he met on bended knee at Venice in 1177. Once Frederick renounced the anti-Popes and gave up the usurped goods and rights of the Church, the Pope lifted the ban of excommunication. Peace with the Lombard League was reached at Constance in 1183. The Pope was conducted back to Rome by imperial troops. In order to prevent a recurrence of disputes in future elections he issued a decree, still in force, making a two-thirds majority the requirement for a valid papal election.

In the following papal reigns, a sort of peace prevailed between the Popes and emperors. Barbarossa complied readily to Pope Clement's call for a Third Crusade, and with the intention of making amends for his previous offences he set out with his armies for the Near East. It was in Cilicia that he met his tragic end in 1190.

Frederick I was succeeded by his son, Henry VI (1190-97), who gained control of Naples and Sicily, thus hemming in the Papal State on all sides. Henry's premature death left as heir to the German throne his three-year old son, the future Frederick II. When he lay dying, Henry asked that Pope Innocent III (1198-1216) preserve the crown for his son. The Emperor's widow, Constance, renewed the old allegiance of the crown to the Papacy, and just before her death, in 1198, she made the Pope her son's guardian. Thus Innocent III administered the kingdoms of Sicily and Naples until his ward attained his majority in 1208.

At his election to the Holy See, Innocent III was only thirty-seven. The poet Walther von der Vogelweide made a now-famous complaint about his great youth. A trained lawyer, theologian and a man of great intellectual gifts, Innocent bent his whole effort toward achieving the complete independence of the Church from secular authority. Neither Gregory, nor Urban, nor Alexander had a loftier conception of the authority of Peter's successor than he did. From the very outset he claimed that the Pope was above all temporal princes. A man of high ideals and great power, Innocent undertook preparations for a new crusade, and did much to further the newly formed and expanding Mendicant Orders of Franciscans and Dominicans (Thomas Aquinas tells Dante of this in the eleventh canto of the *Paradiso* in the *Divina Commedia*).

In 1215 was held the Fourth Lateran Council, the most brilliant of all medieval assemblies; more than twelve hundred prelates and envoys were present. The heretical doctrines of Albigenses and Waldensians were condemned along with the bewildering ideas of Abbot Joachim of Flora. Innocent confirmed the doctrine of transubstantiation, defining it as the true change or metamorphosis of the eucharistic elements of bread and wine in the Blessed Sacrament. Easter Communion became a law binding on all Catholics. And finally, the new orders of monastic life were made subordinate to the Holy See, a decision of the greatest importance for the development of religious life. No council from Nicaea to Trent issued weightier doctrines.

Very soon after his election, Innocent III was called on to resolve the disputed imperial election in Germany. The rival claimants were Philip of Swabia, brother of Henry VI, and Otto of Brunswick. In an effort to maintain the independence and freedom of the Church, the Pope chose the Guelph, Otto, who, unlike the Hohenstaufen rulers, had no claim to Naples or Sicily. But now Otto the Guelph, with no regard for his earlier promises, took up the old Hohenstaufen ideas and prepared to conquer Sicily. Innocent III began to realize how fully he had been deceived. He excommunicated Otto and supported the election of his former ward, the young Hohenstaufen Frederick II. Otto lost all support, and withdrew to his duchy, where he died in 1218.

Innocent also came into sharp conflict in 1206 with King John of England, who was short of land and attempted to occupy the estates of the Primacy of Canterbury by an illegal election. King John refused to accept Stephen Langton, the Archbishop of Canterbury named by the Pope, and refused even to permit his entry into the country. Langton was a professor at the University of Paris and is well known to Biblical scholars as the originator of the chapter divisions of Holy Scripture. When the King refused to yield, Pope

Innocent laid an interdict[43] on England. King John tried to compel the clergy to ignore the interdict; thereupon the Pope excommunicated him, declared him deposed, and entrusted the French king, Philip IV, who was the English King's overlord for his continental possessions, with the carrying out of the sentence. As King Philip IV made preparations for the invasion of England, and as the magnates abandoned him, John yielded to the Pope, became his vassal, surrendered England into the hands of the papal legate and accepted his kingdom from his overlord as a papal fief, at the price of a yearly tribute of seven hundred marks for England and three hundred for Ireland. Hereafter, the Pope supported John against the barons when, in 1215, they forced the terms of *Magna Carta* on the King. Pope Innocent proceeded against them with ecclesiastical penalties, even against Stephen Langton, who made common cause with the barons.

The pontificate of Innocent III is usually considered the high-water mark in papal ascendancy over Europe. He had intervened in the struggle over the German throne; he was feudal overlord of Sicily and England, and since Aragon, Portugal, Hungary and Bulgaria had been established in a kind of feudal relationship with the Holy See, the Pope could for a moment almost be regarded as emperor of Europe. At least all would agree that Innocent belongs among the great historical figures of the world. Simple as he was in his personal life, he had a complete grasp of his function as the successor to St. Peter, and it was he who conceived of the monarchistic view of the Papacy, with Rome in the position of a feudal overlord above all the empires of the world, with the Pope as the true Pontifex Maximus of the Middle Ages, an idea which he represented to the world with dignity and authority. But while we recognize Innocent III as being of the greatest significance for the coming era, we must take with reservations the expressions of amazement in historical writings about Innocent III at the very zenith in the development of papal power. In fact, Innocent was really no more powerful than the Popes before and after him. His financial and military means were modest. Only an unusual set of circumstances brought him into a position where he was able to exercise simultaneous functions as a ruler and as the highest moral authority. It must be kept in mind that the Pope does not possess the material means to enforce this authority where it is not voluntarily recognized: this was exactly the situation of the medieval Popes, even at the time of Innocent III.

In politics, both Popes Honorius III (1216-27) and Gregory IX (1227-41) were constantly at odds with Frederick II (1211-1250), who like all the Hohenstaufens, was brilliant, haughty and treacherous. He governed Sicily well but he is called "the gravedigger of the German Empire." Holding extravagant views of his own power, he was determined to break the power of the Lombard League, and early gains led to greater demands and further aggression. In 1238 the Pope excommunicated and deposed Frederick, who ignored the ban, and marched on Rome, even going so far as to impede the coming of almost a hundred prelates to the Holy City to attend the General Council called by Gregory IX. It is said that they were attacked, murdered or made prisoners at sea by Enzio, Frederick's natural son, and news of these crimes so shocked the aging Pontiff that he died of grief (August, 1241).

His successor, Innocent IV (1243-54), had been a friend of the Emperor Frederick II, and it was hoped his election (which was delayed for a year and a half because Frederick, in control of Rome, refused to permit the exit of two cardinals to attend the solemn conclave, which refused to deliberate without them) would result in a reconciliation. The Pope opened negotiations but Frederick suddenly broke them off and demanded unconditional absolution. When refused, he sent his armies against Rome and his henchmen tried to lay hands on the person of the Pontiff. Innocent fled with his cardinals to Genoa, and then to France, where he was received with the greatest reverence and devotion by St. Louis IX, just then beginning his reign, that career of holiness and knightly chivalry which made him the ideal monarch of the Age of Faith.

Innocent issued the summons for a General Council to be held at Lyons in 1245. Its principal business was the case of the Emperor Frederick, of whom the Pope spoke in his opening address as the greatest enemy of the Church. The Pope preached on the "Five wounds of the Church": the evil conduct of priests and people, the attacks of the Saracens, the Greek schism, the Tartar invasion of Hungary and Frederick's persecution of the Papacy. The defense of Frederick II by his Chancellor was able but made little impression on the Church Fathers, and less on the experienced Pope. The result was a dramatic scene of excommunication and formal deposition by Pope Innocent IV before the entire Council, and with its consent. The solemn cere- mony was carried out with bell, book, candle and all the stately formalities that struck terror into the be- holders. Innocent used to the full the rights which medieval Christendom gave him, and he could hardly have used them on a more cunning, faithless and dan- gerous secular ruler than Frederick II. And the battle was won. Frederick found few to stand by him in Ger- many, which was again plunged into civil war between the papal nominees to succeed him and Frederick's son, Conrad, who attacked them. In spite of, or perhaps because of, repeated acts of cruelty, a blight seems to have fallen on the deposed Emperor's armies. There was a general rising among the Italian cities against him, in which his son Enzio was defeated and captured at Bologna. It was on his way to Enzio's assistance, at the head of his army, that Frederick met death in December, 1250. While he was dying, the Archbishop of Palermo absolved him; Frederick's will shows that at the end he repented and sought to make amends. According to his wish he was buried in Sicily. The Hohenstaufens never recovered from the defeat of Frederick II. After him, other kings who lacked importance were elected and the German kingship survived only as a title.

The short pontificate of Urban IV (1261-64) marks a turning point in the history of the Church and of Europe. To put an end to the insecure situation in Italy, the Pope invited the brother of St. Louis IX of France, the unsaintly Charles of Anjou, to come there and promised to invest him with the kingdoms of Naples and Sicily. Urban never lived to carry out his promise, but the fateful decision had been taken: the Papacy turned away from the German Empire, which had once been its protector but had become its enemy, and veered toward France, which was then the rising great power in Europe.

From the death of Urban IV (1264) to the election of John XXII (1316-34) there were eleven years when the Holy See was unoccupied. Almost none of these intervening Popes were elected in the city of Rome, which fell prey to utter neglect. The city had only a few thousand inhabitants and the Popes resided usually at Perugia or Viterbo; they were almost never in Rome. All these men were, however, highly respected. In happier circumstances, and given a longer period, Pope Gregory X (1271-76) might have gone far to restore the moral prestige of the Papacy. Nevertheless, in this series of papal elections the spirit of the waning thirteenth century was felt. The cardinals, and the princes too, especially the king of Naples, desired "an angel Pope," or an elderly man with as little knowledge of politics as possible. Exaggerated religiosity triumphed in 1294, when after a vacancy of twenty-seven months, the hermit Peter was brought from his cell in the Abruzzi and made Pope as Celestine V. But this man was a genuine saint and soon realized his unfitness for the Papacy. After six months he abdicated. Thus, in the mighty Angevin fortress at Naples, still standing, Cardinal Benedict Gaetano was elected Pope as Boniface VIII (1294-1303). A man of rough violence and a haughty nature, Boniface was one of the unluckiest Popes ever to rule the Church. With the rising tide of the new nationalism, it soon became evident that his ideas concerning papal authority over all crowned heads and peoples belonged to a past age.

The moral supremacy achieved by Innocent III and his successors was not destined to last. The old conflict between the Papacy and the emperors burst forth anew at the end of the thirteenth century, and the outcome was less favorable than before.

With France under a saintly king like Louis IX there was little danger of a break between that country and Rome, but King Philip the Fair (1285-1314) was radically different from his grandfather. Shrewd, calculating, capable and conscientious as a ruler, Philip was far superior to the Pope as a politician. Moreover, he seldom worried about the honesty of his official actions. His policy was to increase the power and greatness of

France. The disputed succession in Scotland, which produced internal confusion, also led to an endless struggle between the kings of France and England, both of whom claimed the Scottish inheritance. Thus Philip was engaged in a war with England under Edward I. The final and most notable feature of this involved situation was the contest with the Papacy, in which both Philip and Edward were involved, and in which the unwise aggression of Boniface VIII reduced his prestige.

In order to continue his policy for France and the war with England, Philip needed money, and found the rights of the Church an important obstacle to his scheme. Without consulting the Pope he levied a tax on the clergy (it was an accepted principle that the clergy made voluntary contributions to the state and met their feudal obligations, but were not compelled to pay extraordinary taxes without the Pope's consent), and terrorized most of them into paying it. When the Cistercian monks appealed to Rome, Pope Boniface rallied to their cause and issued the famous bull, *Clericis Laicos* (1296), in which he forbade any cleric to pay taxes to a civil power without papal consent. Philip the Fair replied by forbidding the export of money from France to Italy, which of course halted the flow of papal revenues to Rome. The Pope was forced to draw back gradually from his position and for a few years there was an uneasy peace, during which Louis IX was canonized a saint.

In 1300, Boniface VIII announced from the loggia of the Lateran Palace the first Jubilee, or Holy Year. (The term "Jubilee" was borrowed from the Old Testament Jobel Year.) There was to be a moratorium of all debts for the occasion, and the faithful were given the opportunity to gain a comprehensive and solemn absolution from guilt, and so far as was within the Church's power, from the punishment due to sin. From all over the Christian world pilgrims streamed to Rome to visit the tombs of the Apostles and gain the jubilee indulgence. For a brief moment, the city of Rome was once again the center of Christendom.

The occasion of the renewal of the struggle between Pope and emperor was Philip's imprisonment of a papal legate, sent to France to remind the king of a proposed crusade. It must be admitted that this legate, Bernard de Saisset, was belligerent in his speech. However, Boniface demanded that he be released. When the King refused, Boniface withdrew the concession on taxation he had made in 1297 and in another bull, *Ausculta Filii* (1301), lectured Philip on his various public crimes, ordered him to appear before a Council of French bishops in Rome to answer certain charges, and threatened him with deposition. Philip replied to the Pope by having one of his counts throw the bull into the fire, by sending out among the people of France a coarse and insulting forgery of it, and by summoning a counter assembly of prelates and nobles to protest against the Pope's usurpation of jurisdiction.

For a time, Philip was restrained by the crushing defeat of his army at Courtrai in 1302. In November, the crowning point of these long conflicts came when Boniface VIII issued the most stunning and controversial papal bull in all history, *Unam Sanctam*, in which he openly referred to the subjection of all temporal authorities to the spiritual power, and repeated the doctrine that the salvation of every human creature turns on his obedience to the Pope. This political theory may have been acceptable four centuries earlier, but uttered at this moment, and so sharply, it could leave the quite dangerous impression that the Pope was claiming the direct power of ruling France. Confronting an unscrupulous and powerfully armed ruler like Philip the Fair, this bold pronouncement could only lead to papal defeat.

Terribly incensed, Philip determined to strike a final blow. After he was excommunicated by Boniface, he sent a force into Italy to arrest the Pope and bring him to France. Wild accusations were made against Boniface before the French Estates General. Few people, even in France, seriously believed them but Boniface had made enemies and thus agitation grew.

The Holy Father was spending a few weeks at the papal villa in Anagni. Sciarra Colonna and William of Nogaret, supporters of Philip, suddenly appeared in the town with a band of five hundred followers. On the fateful day of September 7, 1303, the French broke into the palace, where Boniface met them in full pontifical regalia, with cross in hand. Every abuse was heaped upon the aged Pope; it is said that Colonna even struck him. The defenseless Pope rejected the conditions they laid before him, among which was his abdication. He stood firm against their threats, refusing to repeal his decrees and he replied to these threats with the courageous words: "Here is my neck; here is my head." The French commissioner hesitated. While he deliberated, Nogaret also debated with his henchmen over what to do with the Pope. Three days later the citizens of Anagni rose in revolt, drove out the invaders, and the Pope was saved. He was honorably conducted back to Rome by four hundred Roman knights, and there the eighty-six-year-old Boniface died from the shock, October 11.

The attack on the Pope at Anagni fills the darkest pages in Church history. What was lost was neither the military nor the political power of the Papacy; both were almost nonexistent. A king had defied the Pope openly, and at Anagni the unthinkable had happened —crime and sacrilege. What suffered was the moral prestige of the Papacy. That such an outrage should have happened, and even more that it remained unpunished, shows that on the part of lay rulers religion was becoming a mere activity, arranged like other activities, according to political calculations. "To this extent, Anagni means in Church History the end of the Middle Ages." [44]

XIX

The Popes at Avignon

The thirteenth century marked a great era in the thousand-year history of the Middle Ages. The high point in the medieval idea of the Papacy was reached in the reign of Innocent III, just as medievalism reached its supreme expression in the Gothic cathedrals and its flower of Christian idealism in St. Francis of Assisi. This was the century of Giotto and Dante, of Roger Bacon, of Thomas Aquinas and his rivals, of St. Louis IX in France and his antithesis, Frederick Barbarossa, and Frederick II, the last of the Hohenstaufens. The fourteenth century has no such array of dominant figures. Intellectually exciting, morally decadent, it was an age of pageantry, glitter and romance, when war was followed as the great game of the few, heedless of the many. This was the age of the Avignon Popes; it was followed by a confusion of events which brought about the Great Schism in the West, the Conciliar movement, the Hundred Years' War and the brilliant exploits of the Maid of Lorraine, Joan of Arc; it was also the century of the Black Death (1348), of peasant revolts, and the reaction from which arose the reforming views aired by John Wycliffe.

When Clement V went to Avignon in 1309, Philip IV was still ruling France. During his reign French influence in the Church increased steadily. Many

Frenchmen were elevated to the position of cardinal; for ·example, of the twelve raised to that high office during the brief reign of Celestine V, seven were French, and of the twenty-four cardinals created by Clement V, twenty-three were French.

Benedict XI (1303-04) occupied the See of Peter for a few months after the death of Boniface VIII. The new Pope received the unanimous vote of the cardinals, the last time the French and Italian cardinals would agree for a long interval. By peaceful methods, Benedict tried to win back the stubborn Philip, and showed himself to be a man of courage in excommunicating Sciarra Colonna and Nogaret. So fierce was the resentment of King Philip, however, that he wanted the new Pope to call a council to try the dead Boniface for his alleged misdeeds. Benedict remained steadfast in his refusal. Shortly afterward, he died in Perugia, where the conclave of cardinals assembled to name his successor.

Never had the cardinals been more perplexed over what course they should take. Should they elect an opponent of French policy or someone more favorable to France? On one side, threatening them, stood the supporters of Philip the Fair and the Colonna family, deeply offended by Boniface, and on the other, the friends of the ill-starred Pope. Eleven months went by before an agreement was reached, but at length a middle road was found. The cardinals chose Bertrand de Got, Archbishop of Bordeaux, who was acceptable to Philip and yet was not conspicuous as an enemy of Boniface VIII. Moreover, Bertrand, who styled himself Clement V (1305-14), was not then a subject of France since Bordeaux had been taken by the English in 1303.

The Pope-elect was not at the conclave. When he

received word of his election, instead of going to Rome he summoned the college of cardinals to Lyons where he was consecrated. The papal treasury remained at Assisi. Although Clement intended to go to Rome eventually, he stayed in various cities in France and in 1309 he settled at Avignon in the priory of the Friars Preachers. For seventy years, Rome was not to see another Pope residing permanently there. This period is sometimes referred to as the exile at Avignon, a city which was completely French in language and customs although it belonged to the Queen of Naples. The Avignon residence is also referred to by some writers as "the Babylonian captivity," reminiscent of the Israelites' great exile in Babylonia.

To assuage Philip, who confronted him menacingly, Clement, an invalid racked with all the horrors of a painful cancer, annulled the papal bulls, *Unam Sanctam* and *Clericis Laicos,* as they applied to France, indicating no desire on the Pope's part to challenge the king's temporal authority. The Pope even went so far as to exonerate Philip of all guilt in the affair at Anagni. But when Philip persisted in his demand that Boniface be formally tried and declared an unlawful Pope, Clement refused. Nor did Philip stop here; he added a more dangerous demand—the abolition of the Order of Templars.

This order was founded in Palestine with the encouragement of St. Bernard, and had for its original purpose the defense of the pilgrims on the Crusades. Partly charitable and partly military, the order spread to Europe via Cyprus after the fall of Jerusalem to the Moslems, and gained an enviable reputation for the Templars as bankers, whose great wealth was coveted by Philip. But since their wealth was in the form of Catholic charitable institutions, the King needed the

Pope's co-operation in dissolving the order. In 1307, Philip had all two thousand of the French Templars imprisoned. He brought atrocious charges against them: idolatry, immorality and heresy. He even produced signed confessions wrung from them by torture. Fearful that if he refused to obey Philip, he would be forced to institute proceedings against the late Boniface VIII, the beleaguered Clement called a General Council to Vienne in 1311, in order to shift the responsibility to it. The Council found no justification for condemning the Templars on the evidence presented to them, but under ceaseless pressure from Philip, who was present at the Council, Clement circumvented the Council's decision by issuing an executive decree suppressing the order (a right which every Pope has in regard to any order) on the ground that it had forfeited its good reputation. Many Templars had already been executed; more would follow, including their Grand Master, Jacques de Molay, who was burned at the stake in 1314, maintaining to the end the innocence of his subjects.

The order's property was awarded to the Knights Hospitalers and other military orders but they actually acquired little of it; most of the Templars' holdings passed into the hands of Philip. The destruction of this worthy Order of Templars, against whom no proof of any real crimes was ever produced, is one of the greatest scandals which Church History has to record,[45] and the part that Clement V played in it does no credit to him or his high office. The suppression of the Templars is also an illustration of the power of the new nationalism. There is irony in the fact that the suppression of the Templars was wrung from the Papacy itself; Clement showed himself powerless before Philip and forced to condemn an order whose greatest crime was unswerving fidelity to Rome. Had the Templars, which were in fact regiments of the Pope, been united with the Hospitalers and Teutonic Knights as a papal army, according to the proposal of Boniface and the plan of Innocent III, nationalism might have been held back for centuries.

Two years elapsed after Clement's death before the College of Cardinals could agree on a new Pope. The French cardinals, who had outnumbered the Italians in the Lyons conclave, finally selected Cardinal Jacques d'Euse, Bishop of Avignon, who took the name of John XXII (1316-1334). He was destined to reign as the most important Pope of the fourteenth century, but it was his misfortune to fight a losing battle with the emperor—a battle in which, alas, no great principle was involved. Under him the age-old conflict between emperor and Pope flared up, but the prestige of the Papacy had been fatally weakened.

The occasion for a test of power was another contested election in Germany, where Louis of Bavaria finally gained undisputed power after 1322, but was brushed aside by the Pope, who claimed that the empire was subject to him during the vacancy. He appointed a vicar for the imperial rights in Italy. Louis retaliated by appointing his own vicar, appealed for a General Council and was finally excommunicated in 1324. All the enemies of the Papacy now flocked to the support of Louis, and practically denied the doctrine of the primacy of the Pope. Louis, aware that he had the support of the German princes, declared Pope John a heretic, went to Rome where he received the imperial crown, and set up an anti-Pope. John could do little else; he retaliated by placing all Germany under interdict. When Louis left Rome, the anti-Pope hurried to Avignon to beg the forgiveness of the true Pope.

The contributions John made to ecclesiastical administration, especially in the field of finance, are important and impressive, but his death in 1334 left Germany in a hopelessly entangled situation. Great harm was done to the spiritual life of the Germans under the twenty-year-long interdict and many were convinced that they had been victimized by the French Popes.

Benedict XII (1334-42), a former Cistercian monk, and reformer of both his own and the Benedictine order, succeeded Pope John XXII. He would have been happy to end the quarrel with Louis the Bavarian but he was thwarted by the French King, who was not anxious to see a papal reconciliation with Germany, and the return of the curia to Rome. Benedict, meanwhile, began to build the majestic Palace of the Popes at Avignon, one of the great monuments of late Gothic, which still stands as a reminder of the city's former splendor. The cathedral church which stands nearby appears small and unimportant in comparison to the castle. This contrast typifies the Avignon epoch: "the recession of the ecclesiastical element and the predominance of the worldly, warrior-prince forces."[46] The unending quarrel with Germany resulted in 1338 in the "Golden Bull," the declaration of the German princes at Rhens-on-the-Rhine that the German Emperor was elected by them; both he and the Empire were independent of the Papacy. It also set down who should administer the imperial power during a vacancy. Innocent VI (1352-62), who was then Pope, did not protest. Thus the Papacy lost one of its important political powers, and its prestige was further weakened.

Clement VI (1342-52) purchased Avignon and its surrounding territory for the Papal States. Urban V (1362-70) visited Rome briefly but found it so turbulent that he returned to Avignon to die. Cardinal Albornoz was dispatched to restore order in the Papal State in Italy. When he died (1367) much had been accomplished there. Papal legates regulated the unsettled conditions as well as could be done, and thus helped to remove the obstacles to the Pope's resuming residence in the Holy City. For the Pope was now being urged from all sides to return to the city of Peter, by Petrarch, the great Latinist and forerunner of the Italian renaissance, and the saintly Bridget of Sweden, who made numerous pilgrimages to Rome, wrote letters of remarkable candor to overcome the doubts of the new Pope, Gregory XI (1370-78), and finally settled in Rome near its holy shrines.

To be sure, Avignon had certain advantages. The terms "exile" and "Babylonian captivity" are unfortunate, for the Popes were more securely and comfortably sheltered in France than in Rome, where they were tormented by Orsinis, Colonnas, Guelphs and Ghibellines. France was in every respect, including the intellectual, the leading power in the West. Moreover, Avignon could be reached from anywhere without crossing the Alps. But all of this does not outweigh the plain fact that Rome was the city of Peter, the city that houses the tombs of the martyrs, the center of a thousand-year tradition. The Pope is the head of the Church because he is the successor of St. Peter, as first bishop of Rome. The Papacy is an international institution, not a French administrative machine. For a period of seventy years, some seven Popes ruled the Church from Avignon—but their absence did not spell an end to disturbances in Italy, especially in Florence. Pope Gregory XI had to send Breton mercenaries to Italy to quell them.

St. Bridget died without having the desire of her heart fulfilled, but at that time there lived in Siena a pious virgin, Catherine Benincasa, a great mystic, who was also very intelligent. Her sole concern was for the Church. This holy woman, who was not a nun but a Dominican Tertiary, used her prestige and influence, which was very strong among the Florentines, and wrote numerous letters to reconcile the Republic of Florence with the Pope, making possible his return to Rome. From Italy came the voice of the one really great personage produced during this wretched century to strengthen the Pope's will: "Go, restore the greatness of Rome, that garden which was and is even now sprinkled with the blood of martyrs. Rome still has need of martyrs." Of course, there were other considerations which moved Gregory XI to return to Rome, but even contemporaries regarded the voice of St. Catherine of Siena as a divine summons, and have attributed to her the chief merit for Gregory's decision. On September 13, 1376, the Pope left Avignon forever, and on January 17 of the following year, he was able to make his entry into Rome. The Avignon Papacy had come to an end.

XX

The Great Western Schism

Gregory XI died fourteen months after his return
to Rome, which had been somewhat premature since
all Italy was now stirred up, disorganized, and cities
like Cesena were virtually laid waste by marauding
troops. Around the Vatican, where the sacred conclave was in session, mobs crowded the square of St.
Peter's and howled: "Elect an Italian or you die." The
sixteen terrified cardinals, only four of whom were
Italians, hastily elected Bartolomeo Prignano, the Nea-
politan Archbishop of Bari, who as Urban VI (1378-
79) was the first Italian Pope elected in seventy-four
years.

While the Pope-elect, who was then in Rome, was
on his way to the Vatican, the mob rushed into the
Papal palace demanding to know the new Pope's name.
The cardinals told them to go to St. Peter's. The multi-
tude thought they said: "the cardinal of St. Peter's,"
who happened to be Cardinal Tebaldeschi, an octo-
genarian Roman.

Believing their lives endangered, the cardinals hastily
dressed this old man in papal vestments, seated him
on the papal throne and then they fled. The Cardinal
vainly tried to explain to the excited crowd that not he
but Archbishop Prignano had been duly elected.

The following day, in a calmer atmosphere, the city
magistrate explained what had happened, and Arch-

147

bishop Prignano was duly consecrated Urban VI. Father Hughes concludes that in the circumstances of his election there was enough of a case against its validity to exploit it, should it be anyone's desire to do so, and soon it was very much the desire of a great many people to be rid of Urban by any possible means.[47]

The new Pope proceeded to purge the curia of many abuses which had been justly criticized but his methods were harsh, tactless and tyrannical. He was crude in his treatment of the French cardinals who still longed for Avignon. He had an explosive temper, and some have even thought that his mind was deranged. We find the saintly Catherine of Siena writing to Urban: "For the love of Jesus crucified, Holy Father, soften a little the sudden movements of your temper." [48] Some of the cardinals soon regretted their decision to elect Urban, and fled to Anagni. From there they announced that the election of Urban had been forced on them by the threats of the Roman mob and was therefore invalid. The Papacy was vacant. Proceeding to a new election they named Cardinal Robert of Geneva, a Frenchman who commanded the papal armies and who styled himself Clement VII. All the cardinals, with one exception, recognized Clement as Pope. After his consecration he returned to Avignon, and thus began the Great Western Schism destined to last for almost forty years.

Some argue that the chief cause of the schism was the extreme nationalism of the French cardinals. Yet it became very difficult for Christians to decide on which side rested the right. We now know that the election of Urban VI was legitimate and valid; fear of the mob only hastened the election, but it did not dictate the choice. The cardinals feared they had elected an unacceptable candidate, which goes far toward an explanation of the Tebaldeschi "comedy of errors." At the time, however, some of the greatest minds and even great theologians and saints were unable to agree on their allegiance to the true Pope. Christendom was divided into what are called the *Two Obediences*. Both camps were equally representative of the Church, some supporting the Avignon Pope and others his Roman antagonist; the two claimants had nearly equal support. St. Vincent Ferrer and St. Colette supported Clement, while St. Catherine of Siena was one of Urban's staunchest defenders. Clement generally claimed the loyalty of South Italy, Spain, Scotland and France, while Urban's strength was to be found in Portugal, Norway, Denmark, Sweden, Germany, Poland, Hungary, England, Ireland and North Italy. Christendom, as can be seen, was divided along lines more or less political, according as its sympathies were French or anti-French.

Adherents to the Popes at Avignon and Rome were sincere in their convictions, and the people of Europe could only accept the decisions of their leaders in offering loyalty to one Pope or another. There was, however, no falling away from the Faith, no heretical doctrine, no rebellion against recognized authority. There was no immediate harm to the care of souls. The validity of priestly orders and of the sacraments was not affected by the so-called schism. Strictly speaking, there was no real schism for a schism is regarded as a rebellion against an admittedly lawful Pope, whereas in this case there was full agreement as to the powers and obedience due to a lawful Pope. The trouble was, no one could be certain who was the true successor of Peter. The division was not a real schism therefore, but it was a very real division, its effects were unfortunate for the Church, and it lasted for almost forty years.

The spectacle of two claimants to Peter's throne represented a sad state of affairs and created unending confusion. Whole countries, Christians everywhere and even religious orders were divided and ranged against each other. This rivalry was reminiscent of disputed elections within the Holy Roman Empire, and it weakened the authority and prestige of the Pope. Not indifference, but religious overexcitement resulted; fantastic plans for reform appeared. Moreover, the attempt to restore unity resulted in an attack on the Papal supremacy and in an even more confusing election of a third claimant to the papal throne.

The Church by no means acquiesced in the division; from the first realization that it existed, schemes were put forth by both factions for reunion. Some embraced the idea that a general council should be called to deal with the matter, assume final authority, depose the rival claimants to the Holy See, and elect a true successor to it. Extremists began to teach that the ultimate authority in the Church rested in the episcopate, or representatives from the Church meeting in council. This theory is known as conciliarism.

John Gerson, chancellor of the University of Paris, went even further. His heretical notion was that not bishops alone, nor even priests, but all the baptized faithful were the real sources of papal authority. In a general council, he claimed, every Catholic should have the right to vote. Another current of opinion argued, why only two Popes? Why not one for each country?

Both Urban VI and Clement VII were dead by 1394. This afforded an excellent opportunity for the cardinals to end the schism but strong convictions in both groups prevented agreement. The Avignon anti-

Popes, Clement and Benedict, were men of ability but obstinate in persisting in separation, even though prior to his election Benedict had promised, if chosen Pope, to work for reunion. The Roman successors to Urban were Boniface IX, Innocent VII and Gregory XII. It was during the reign of Gregory XII (1406-15) that the movement to end the division really began. At the time of his election, all the participating candidates among the College of Cardinals stated their willingness, if elected, to resign *if* the Avignon Pope would do likewise.

Two more years passed in futile efforts to arrange a meeting between the two rivals. The French King now abandoned the Avignon Pope, declared himself neutral and turned the whole question over to the University of Paris, which proposed three solutions. The last of these called for a general council, which is a legally assembled meeting of dignitaries and skilled theologians acting in behalf of the Church, for the purpose of discussing and defining matters of doctrine and Church discipline. But such a council cannot act independently of the Pope; it must be approved by him, and presided over by him or his delegate. Its decisions are binding only with the approval of the Roman Pontiff.

The growing party of neutrals sent letters inviting attendance at the Council, which met in Pisa in 1409. Neither Gregory nor Benedict appeared at Pisa and neither approved of the Council, which made it invalid. Nevertheless, those in attendance proceeded to depose both Popes, after condemning them for schism, heresy and perjury, and they elected a third Pope, the Archbishop of Milan, who took the name of Alexander V. Now this scandalous situation was more confused than ever. After Alexander's death, within the year, Baldassare Cossa, who took the name John XXIII, succeeded him and proceeded to heap further disgrace on this already much disgraced office. This trader in indulgences and ecclesiastical financier, who was a former pirate, invited the scorn of everyone, even those responsible for his election. At length, the Holy Roman Emperor, Sigismund, intervened and forced on John the calling of a new Council which met at Constance in 1414, put a virtual end to the schism and brought a culmination to the disgraceful chaos of forty years.

Never had this German town bordering on Lake Constance seen such an assembly as descended on it from all points that November: 29 cardinals, 185 bishops, 300 doctors of theology, over 100 abbots and hundreds of other theologians, canonists and ambassadors of princes. The dominant figure was the Emperor —whose prestige and power backed the Council when it declared John deposed, and declared null and void the decrees of any Pope who failed to submit to it. Having fled the city, in a most unseemly fashion, John was then captured and placed under guard. Six days after his deposition he added his own act of resignation.

The eighty-year-old Roman claimant, Gregory XII, finally decided to abdicate on condition that the Council accord him the right of officially convoking it. This was granted but there still remained in distant Spain the obdurate Benedict XIII, the heir of the Pope who had begun the schism. He retaliated to the Council's condemnation of him by threats of excommunication to the churchmen and deposition to the princes, but his fulminations went unheeded since his supporters had dwindled to a mere handful. The Council spent a total of two years in its deliberations and finally, on St. Martin's Day, a conclave of twenty-three cardinals elected their fellow cardinal, Odo Colonna, Pope for the whole Church. This was November 11, 1417. The new Pope took the name Martin V (1417-31) and the schism came to an end.

In another of its decrees, the Council of Constance asserted the supremacy of the council over the Pope. Conciliarism was still alive. The Council of Basel (1431-39) refused to be dissolved at the command of Pope Eugene IV (1431-47); instead it decreed that the council was superior to the Pope and elected the last anti-Pope in history. The Council at Ferrara almost succeeded in healing the Greek schism. Actually, however, the conciliar movement lost support after Constance. Popular interest in Church councils waned and Popes grew increasingly suspicious of them. Finally, after the theory of conciliarism had discredited itself, Pope Pius II condemned it in 1460.

Only one thing—the ending of the Great Western Schism—was accomplished by the Church councils of the fifteenth century. Heresy persisted. And so did the need for a thorough reform of the Church. The spirit which had produced the reforms of the eleventh century, or which in the high Middle Ages had animated the Cistercians and Friars, was now lacking.[49]

Midway through this unhappy century came the terrible catastrophe of the "Black Death." This was the contemporary phrase for the bubonic plague, brought to Europe from India and China by trading ships. Those who were attacked by this highly contagious disease died within hours. There was no known remedy, and no country of Europe escaped its devastation, not even Iceland or Greenland. From Italy in 1438, it spread through Spain, southern France, Bavaria, the Rhineland, and by the summer of that same year it had reached England, where half the population perished in twelve months. The mortality was incredible.

The plague carried off a quarter or more of the French population. At Avignon, for example, in addition to a whole variety of other charities, organized on a lavish scale, the Pope handed over papal lands for a special cemetery, and in six weeks eleven hundred corpses had been buried in it. No class suffered more than the clergy, who were remarkably faithful to their duty, but the consequence of such devastation was a shortage of priests afterward, and the depleted ranks were filled with untrained and unsuitable subjects. However, the total effect of this pestilence can merely be grasped, never exaggerated. Students of secular history will notice that it broke the spirit of the generation upon which it fell. "The temptation to despair of the spiritual and live only for the day seized many of the survivors." A new spirit of carelessness and of reckless defiance of divine truth and Church teachings was abroad.

One evidence of the decline of Christian faith is the popularity of John Wycliffe (1324-84), "the day's one real heretic." Wycliffe was an English scholar-priest who wanted to rebuild Christianity on the sole basis of Scripture as a rule of faith. He attacked the authority of the Pope, severely condemned certain laxities in the lives of the clergy, and dismissed hierarchy, priesthood and sacraments as all mere human inventions. The Church, he taught, must return to its first state of simple poverty. This revolutionary doctrine, preached in England by the Lollards for some forty years (1376-1415), continued to linger on in remote corners of the country for almost a century. It was also carried into Bohemia, where it found an able apostle in John Huss (1369-1415), who secured a large following. The Hussites were the real influence in the heresy's adoption in Bohemia, where it became an additional means of self-expression for the nationalist anti-German movement of the Czechs.

Wycliffe was condemned by local synods in England; he ceased to preach publicly and died unmolested. John Huss was condemned by the Council of Constance and burned at the stake. Ever since his death he has been the great hero of his race.[50] A crusade had to be preached against the Hussites, who carried on in the spirit of their martyred leader. Wycliffites in England were also punished, but both groups persisted in forming an undercurrent of heretical opposition.

Continued possession of lands in southwestern France by the Kings of England, and English claims to still other French provinces once held by the English crown served as a serious handicap to the full development of a centralized French monarchy. A disputed succession to the French throne and various other minor irritations contributed to the outbreak of a series of wars in 1340, fought intermittently for a whole century. The issues over which these wars were fought were settled only after that long period of time, hence the name, the Hundred Years' War (1337-1453). At the battle of Crécy (1346) the English infantrymen, with their "long bows," mowed down the feudal cavalry on which the French mainly relied. Ten years later the "Black Prince" inflicted another defeat on the French at Poitiers (1356).

Despite the truce of 1360, the war continued. In 1415, Henry V of England took advantage of the civil war in France to invade Normandy and crush the French troops at Agincourt. Henry then proceeded to capture Rouen and soon mastered all of Normandy. The terms of the peace treaty were most humiliating to the French: the unfortunate French King, Charles VI, who had been overcome by insanity in 1392, was to be succeeded at his death, not by his son, the Dauphin, but by Henry V of England. The Dauphin, however, refused to recognize this Treaty of Troyes which disinherited him. Though slight, frail and bow-legged, Charles VII, as he styled himself, somehow earned the title "the Well-served." The first to serve him well was the Maid of Lorraine, Joan of Arc.

As early as 1424 Joan, the daughter of Jacques Darc (later changed to d'Arc) first heard the angelic voices, calling her to free France from the English intruders. But it was not until 1429 that she secured the audience with the Dauphin at Chinon in which she persuaded him of her divine commission. Then, armed and mounted, she went forth, God's miracle, to answer the summons of her divine command. She set a new tone; and by urging action, and more action, she raised the morale of the French troops who, though skeptical at first, were convinced that they now had the aid of a saint. "This young girl, who came to fight at the moment when all seemed lost . . . found faith and secret hope among her people, raised them up, and made them follow her. After that she could well submit, suffer and die. For all time she had triumphed."

XXI

The Renaissance

The Renaissance is rightly regarded as the greatest cultural revival in European history. More than that, the term covers the many aspects of change—economic, social, political and intellectual—that made this one of the most exciting eras in the history of Western civilization. Yet we must keep in mind that the Renaissance was mainly an artistic revival.

The Papacy, as we have seen, had survived a major crisis during which its position in the Church was under almost constant attack. The Popes of the later Middle Ages necessarily felt obliged to devote much energy to defending and maintaining their position in Italy. They did succeed in preserving their constitutional rights despite attacks. However, they failed to retain their leadership throughout Europe during this critical period, which saw the advance of heresy in England and Bohemia and which heard the rumblings of discontent elsewhere. The Renaissance Popes concentrated on preserving their Papal State in Italy and patronizing the arts and letters. The former task, given the political conditions of the time, was perhaps an essential one but the methods employed to hold and increase the papal territory were scarcely different from those of Italian despots. In their patronage of the arts and letters the Popes devoted time, energies and money, at the expense of the urgent needs of the Church as

157

a whole. A pagan spirit affected the Renaissance in the later fifteenth century. Worldly considerations of government, and even of art, often took precedence over spiritual interests.

In the later Middle Ages, scholars, princes and many churchmen were enthusiastic in their devotion to the classical literature and language of Greek and Roman antiquity. Interest in the classics had not been lacking during the Middle Ages, but at the height of the Renaissance in Italy the invention of movable type and the printing press did much to spread the movement, with its accompanying classicism, and to render it fashionable and influential in Western Europe. The Renaissance man studied classical civilization, and the application of classical ethics and its mode of living to everyday affairs. He paid particular attention to the "human side of life" and the frank enjoyment of the good things of this world, so well exemplified in the writings of Graeco-Roman antiquity. This study of the classics for their intrinsic values and this preoccupation with the individual in this world led to a new exaltation of man, known as humanism.

There was nothing new in this revival of learning and letters. Latin literature had formed the basis of most medieval education. There had been other revivals in the twelfth and thirteenth centuries; indeed, some regard the Renaissance as simply a culmination of a series of revivals which began in the ninth century with Charlemagne. Now, however, there was a different emphasis in the Renaissance scholar's attitude toward classical culture. While he did not always abandon his faith in Christianity or deny the supernatural, he so revered the purely human that the spiritual ideals of the Middle Ages were inevitably undermined. Humanism resulted in a reaction against asceticism and other-worldliness. Humanists were not heretics, but there was a good deal in the atmosphere and spirit of Renaissance scholarship that was pagan. Therefore the Church's position was somewhat difficult, but the new learning was accepted even by the Papacy itself.

During the Renaissance there was a marked disposition to repudiate medieval culture, whose art was now described as "Gothic" or barbarous. Because Aristotle was associated with medieval Scholasticism, the humanists made Plato their idol and neo-Platonism deeply influenced Renaissance thought.

In Italy, the most culturally advanced of all European countries, the Renaissance began. First among the early humanists was Petrarch (1304-1374), whose absorbing passion for Latin literature prompted him to reconstruct the form and style of the pure Latin tongue as written and spoken by Cicero and the ancient Romans, and to collect the works of the great Roman writers. While Petrarch was an admirer of pagan life, and is sometimes called "the father of humanism," he was not anti-Christian. On the contrary, he assailed heretics, pleaded for the Popes to return to Rome from Avignon and received most of the honors and sinecures within the power of the Popes to bestow.

Italian humanism was enriched by the arrival of Byzantine scholars like Manuel Chrysoloras (d. 1415), who taught the Greek language at the University of Florence. That brilliant city became the center of the cultural Renaissance and the refuge for other Byzantine artists and scholars who came to Italy after the fall of Constantinople in 1453.

Like many another tyrant, Lorenzo de Medici, or Lorenzo "the Magnificent," of Florence will be long remembered for his patronage of the arts rather than for his political intrigues and oppression. Cosimo de Medici, another member of this wealthy house of Florentine bankers, showed so much intelligent interest in various aspects of Renaissance art and letters that he amassed a collection of books and manuscripts which formed the nucleus for the Medici Library, the most famous in Europe. Under the patronage of the Medici, a "Platonic" academy was also instituted in Florence, boasting in its membership such outstanding humanists as Marsiglio Ficino and Pico della Mirandola.

Pope Nicholas V (1447-55) has been referred to as "the first humanist Pope," and it is certainly true that he first brought humanism to the Vatican. He desired to see Rome the center of the new learning, the new culture, the new art. Fifty years after his death it was all this. We owe to Pope Nicholas the foundation of the celebrated Vatican Library. He set out to preserve the remains of Roman buildings and monuments. On the advice of Alberti that old St. Peter's was unsafe, Pope Nicholas undertook the construction in the classical Renaissance style of a colossal new structure—barely initiated when he died. It was to become the greatest church in Christendom.

This staggering project was carried on intermittently during three centuries (1420-1626). Pope Julius II selected Bramante's design. The cornerstone was laid in 1506 to house Michelangelo's tomb of Julius II. The work was continued by San Gallo, Fra Giocondo and Raphael. Michelangelo became chief architect in 1546 and restored Bramante's original plan, laying out the enormous 450-foot dome over the Greek cross. During the baroque period, Bernini designed the long colonnades which extended forward from the sides, ending in semicircles enclosing the square. The dedication of St. Peter's Cathedral by Pope Urban VIII came in 1626.

Another talented humanist was Aeneas Sylvius Piccolomini, whose private life had been more scandalous than most figures in the revival. Then, at forty, he reformed, received Holy Orders and diverted his genius to the service of religion. He was elected Pope, and as Pius II (1458-64) he found an unavoidable Italian war absorbing the energies he would have preferred to direct toward the recovery of Constantinople. He was the last of the crusading Popes. He stood ready to sell manuscripts and chalices to provide funds for the crusade. After pleading and negotiating with the Catholic princes during his entire reign, he finally assembled an army and a fleet, the best he could do, but not sufficient to oppose the might of that brilliant Turkish leader, Mohammed II. The Pope died upon arrival at Ancona, after the old man had traveled so far to take his share in the hardship of the expedition.

Sixtus IV (1471-84) restored and beautified Rome, built the Sistine Chapel, reorganized the Vatican Library and lavished money and honors on humanist scholars brought to Rome.

However, if Pope Nicholas V made Rome the center of the new learning, it also became the center of the new vices, and some of the Popes were their foremost practitioners. This very Pope Sixtus IV introduced the evil of nepotism into the papal court and lowered the whole tone of the Sacred College of Cardinals by his bad appointments. Innocent VIII (1484-92) became Pope through simony. The notorious Borgia Pope, Alexander VI (1492-1503), was elected through bribery and became the source of the greatest scandals in all Renaissance history. With his death the peculiarly immoral life of the papal court came to an end. His rehabilitation, said Pastor, "is a hopeless task."

Julius II (1503-13) demonstrated ability as one of the most vigorous of all European rulers. A first class diplomatist and a really great general (he rarely removed his riding boots, even for pontifical occasions!), he is not exactly the example of a model Pope, but he seemed to be the type needed during those turbulent times. He finally crushed the Roman barons and reorganized the Papal States for the first time with the Pope as their effective ruler. He was fierce, driving and inflexible. Like the Tudor king, Henry VII, he furthered his policy by marriage alliances. In addition to encouraging the monastic orders, he contributed heavily to the beautification of Rome.

The successor to Julius II was the cardinal, Giovanni de Medici, Pope Leo X (1513-21), whose career epitomized the Renaissance in all its tendencies. The fact that he was head of the newly restored ruling family of Florence meant that for the best part of twenty years Medici Popes would rule and fight, not so much for the Holy See as for the interests of the Medici family. They left the Papacy the least trusted of all the sovereignties in Western Europe.

In a sense the printing press formed a link between the humanism of Italy and the humanism of the northern countries. North of the Alps there was knowledge of the new learning before the appearance of the Gutenberg Bibles, but the first half of the sixteenth century was the golden age of northern humanism, which had a more distinctly religious slant than its counterpart in the south. Here there was manifested less interest in classical learning for its own sake, so characteristic of Italy, and a greater desire to direct the cultural revival into channels of educational and religious reform. For example, Johann Reuchlin (d. 1522) studied Hebrew in Italy under Pico della Mirandola and then devoted himself to a critical study of the text of the Old Testament.

"The prince of humanists" was Desiderius Erasmus (1466-1536), a native of Rotterdam who also became preoccupied with Church reform after studying among the Brethren of the Common Life at Deventer. As a monk, Erasmus became so absorbed in the new learning that he asked for a dispensation from his vows to devote his time to scholarship, writing, counseling and corresponding with princes and lay rulers. In this way he became a welcome guest at the courts of Europe and universities everywhere. Erasmus spent many years in England, where he formed a close friendship with two leading humanists, John Colet and Thomas More. To the latter he dedicated his famous book, *In Praise of Folly,* in which he demonstrated wit, gentle satire directed against decadent Scholasticism, corrupt and ignorant clergymen, the foibles and hypocrisies of monks, and a great deal more. In addition to his wide travels, voluminous correspondence, his satirical *Colloquies,* and his classical commentaries, Erasmus was also a Biblical scholar who contributed a critical edition of the Greek New Testament. Erasmus represents the golden mean, a true Renaissance man achieving at once high standards of scholarship and maintaining traditional concepts of Christian morality.

The Renaissance was a great deal more than a revival of pagan learning. There was an impressive record of new achievements in art, literature, science, philosophy, politics, education and religion. As it happened, the achievements in painting, science and politics bore little resemblance to the classical heritage.

In painting and sculpture the Renaissance spirit rises to its greatest heights. Glories existed that made the Quattrocento, or the fifteenth century, impressively important in the history of art. The majority of the painters of the Quattrocento were Florentine. Through such overwhelming personalities as Leonardo da Vinci, Michelangelo and Raphael, the century was enriched with masterpieces rarely equaled and never surpassed, especially in their portrayal of spiritual qualities.

Masaccio, although he died at the age of twenty-seven, inspired the work of other Italian painters for a hundred years. Michelangelo's giant forms show his genius in forcing the dying Gothic content through the medium of classic forms, thus combining the idealism of antiquity with the profoundly religious spirit of the man himself. His magnificent work on the ceiling of the Sistine Chapel from 1508 to 1512 is the greatest single-handed accomplishment in the history of art.

One of the most intellectual painters of all times, and most versatile was the great Leonardo da Vinci (1452-1519) but Raphael (1483-1520) was certainly the most popular artist of the entire Renaissance. He devoted himself to the cultivation of an ideal type of beauty as an end in itself and also he worked toward the expression of religious sentiments. Like other painters of the time, such as Ghirlandaio, da Vinci, Perugino and Caravaggio, Raphael showed worldly tendencies. He has been accused of sometimes painting like a pagan. Perugino was charged with being an atheist; Caravaggio, the great naturalist, used a drowned woman as a model for his "Death of the Blessed Virgin Mary" (now in the Louvre); and Veronese was hauled before the court of the Inquisition for using irrelevant detail. Albrecht Dürer (1471-1528), under the influence of these Italian masters, was the best representative of German art at this time.

It was Pope Eugene IV who first brought Fra Angelico (1387-1455) to Rome to decorate the Chapel of the Blessed Sacrament. The frescoes of this artist, who gave bodily form to visions of spiritual loveliness, as for example those in the Dominican monastery of San Marco in Florence, stand out as perhaps the highest expression of mystical art.

Toward the end of the century, agitation was stirred up by the teachings of Girolamo Savonarola (1452-98), a Dominican monk in Florence and Prior of San Marco. He not only introduced strict reforms into his monastery but he undertook to preach publicly, with the ardor of a prophet, against the corruption in the Church, especially among the clergy. There is no question of his virtue and strict orthodoxy. He denounced the corrupt court of Lorenzo de Medici and with the aid of the French King, Charles VIII, he was successful in expelling the Medici from Florence, which he ruled for a while as a religious dictator, actually effecting a great moral improvement. But when he censured Pope Alexander VI from the pulpit he was summoned to Rome for his continued disobedience. Savonarola was excommunicated in 1497. He claimed the ban was fraudulent, disregarded it, continued preaching and appealed from the authority of the Pope to a future Council of the Church. Abandoned by his followers and imprisoned, Savonarola continued to insist that he was divinely commissioned by God and was willing to go through the ordeal by fire (a process defying all justice was initiated against him). Pope Alexander VI vainly tried to bring the affair to Rome for settlement. Through terrible tortures, Savonarola was forced to repudiate his claim that he was a messenger of God. In 1498 he and two other Dominicans were condemned to the gallows in Florence and their corpses were publicly burned. Even to this day opinions regarding Savonarola are divided. Several Popes, and St. Philip Neri, a native of Florence, revered him as martyr and saint.

So the troubled century came to an end. The final break between Greeks and Latins had been made; the invasion of Italy by Charles VIII led to a bitter Franco-Spanish feud. Churchmen disputed over vital issues. The Bohemians never forgot the burning of Huss. The century-long struggle between France and England made Joan a martyr. The apathetic West saw Constantinople fall after a final successful Turkish siege. Gallicanism broke out—the extension of the policy of individual arrangements between the Papacy and nation-states, as, e. g., the Pragmatic Sanctions of Bourges and Mainz. And, as Savonarola had foretold, the postponement of reform was about to put the Church to a severe test.

Leo X, a good-living cleric, strict with himself about such matters as fasting and the priestly obligations of his position in life, was a true man of the Renaissance in his classical culture, his taste for the arts, and his fondness for associating with artists and men of letters. In what was perhaps his greatest ambition, to see Rome the acknowledged center of European culture, he was successful. He continued to encourage Raphael's painting and Bramante's work on the new St. Peter's. He gave the cardinal's hat to the humanist scholar, Bembo, and he promoted Greek studies in the Roman University.[51] But the really great event in his eight-year reign was the outbreak of the Protestant revolt, which he is reputed to have shrugged off as a squabble between two German monks. When Leo died the Protestant revolt was rapidly gathering momentum. For years, Catholics, lay and clerical, and many northern humanists had been calling for a reformation "in head and members," within the Church. Now men stood ready, as Goethe put it, to tear asunder the seamless robe of Christ.

XXII

The Protestant Revolt

The events of the fourteenth century and the scandals of the fifteenth caused the Pope further loss of prestige, especially as he continued to engage in political activity. But the spiritual power of the Papacy survived. By 1500, extreme solutions to reconcile the two powers, civil and ecclesiastical, seemed to be a matter of time. At this moment, Luther's appearance on the scene and the coincidence of other unexpected events led to the revolt from Christian unity of a large part of Europe.

The rebellion, however, was mainly of state against Church. Clerical shortcomings, it is true, were widespread, and in the case of the Great Schism or the Renaissance Popes, distinctly spectacular. However, these abuses were slowly being checked. Unfortunately they were still so patent as to give occasion to and apology for rebellion. Complaints about abuses were especially rife in Germany where a widespread and permanent revolt developed against the Church. There pamphleteers complained that the country was being drained of money to support a corrupt papal court in Rome.

In every Christian land, but particularly in Germany, protests were registered against the practice of bestowing high Church offices and lands on absentee Italian churchmen. Thus we can more readily understand Luther's amazing popular appeal which accounts in part for his success. Whereas formerly tendencies to rebellion remained leaderless, now the abuses of ecclesiasticism, the loss of prestige suffered by the Papacy, the adventurous impulses of the Renaissance, the ease with which new ideas could be spread with the new discovery of printing all combined against the Church. Added to this was the growing power and self-consciousness of national states and their rulers, who coveted the temporal powers of the Papacy and the Church's wealth and who would go to any lengths, even a religious revolt to consolidate their own position. It follows that the success of Luther, after the failure of various premature reformers, was mainly due to the ripeness of time. Where the revolt against the Catholic Church was successful it led to a nationalistic concept of religion.

The event which provided the spark setting off the chain of events culminating in the Protestant revolt occurred in Germany in 1517 and it concerned indulgences. Ever since the Crusades the Pope had been dispensing indulgences, by virtue of the authority conferred by Christ on St. Peter to hold and use "the keys of the kingdom of heaven," and "to bind and loose" on earth. These indulgences, according to Catholic teaching, were a plea for removal of the punishment to be meted out to a person after death for sins for which he had repented on earth. By means of the indulgence, punishment in Purgatory might be taken away wholly or partially. Pope Urban had granted a plenary or full indulgence for knights who were killed fighting in the Crusades.

Now, in 1517, Pope Leo X was eager to rebuild St. Peter's Cathedral, a task already begun but immensely expensive. When the Archbishopric of Magdeburg fell vacant, the young Archbishop of Mainz virtually bought the plural office with its rich holdings for ten thousand ducats, most of which he borrowed from the Fugger bankers of Augsburg. Pope Leo X gave the Archbishop something like a monopoly for the preaching of indulgences in Germany to enable him to repay his loan. Agents of the papacy, including the Dominican monk, Johan Tetzel, were sent into the German states, where they employed methods not unlike those of high-pressure salesmanship. Tetzel came within forty kilometers of the University of Wittenberg, where Martin Luther (1483-1546), an Augustinian monk, was professor of theology. This led the vigorous, knowledgeable, ambitious young monk to question the tactics of Tetzel and the whole doctrine of the Church concerning indulgences. He posted ninety-five theses or assertions on the church door at Wittenberg in 1517, and challenged any theologian to debate them with him. The theses were translated from Latin to German and circulated through much of Germany, where they provoked spirited discussion. But Luther went further than this. For some years he had been a close student of the Pauline epistles, as well as the writings of St. Augustine. From these two sources he found a basis for the conviction that man is so sinful as to be totally incapable of doing "good works" and achieving salvation. Only by faith in God and his infinite mercy can man attain salvation. This was Luther's ultimate doctrine of salvation, or "justification by faith," in opposition to the traditional Catholic doctrine of salvation through faith, the sacraments and good works. This doctrine was questioned along with the teaching on indulgences in Luther's *Ninety-Five Theses*.

In a debate with the eminent theologian, Johann Eyck, Luther was maneuvered into the admission that some of his views were identical with those of Johann Huss, condemned as a heretic in 1415. Then Luther published three provocative pamphlets attacking the privileged position of the clergy, the authority of the Papacy, the sacramental system and other Church teachings. He appealed to the nationalism and ambition of the German nobility and pointed shrewdly to the wealth of the Church which they might appropriate. He urged a break with the Church's authority and the elimination of foreign control. At the Diet of Worms, in the presence of the Holy Roman Emperor, Charles V, his troops, many high Church dignitaries and papal legates (after Luther had refused to answer the summons to Rome), Luther acknowledged the pamphlets were his and refused to deny the beliefs they contained. This Diet of Worms, which witnessed Luther's electric defiance, also witnessed the manifest division of the Catholics, the bishops wholly indifferent, or as the Papal Legate reported, trembling like rabbits before a trap.[52]

In 1521 Pope Leo excommunicated Luther; the Diet ordered the burning of his works and declared him an outlaw. However, he was protected from the troops of the Emperor and the courts of the Church by the Elector of Saxony and was conducted to the impregnable castle of the Wartburg, where he devoted the next two years to a German translation of the Bible. What the Papacy had earlier scoffed at as a mere squabble among monks had now developed into a full-scale religious revolt with heavy economic and political overtones, for the political situation favored Luther. Within a few years his teaching had spread like wildfire over northern and central Germany. As Professor Carlton Hayes has observed, Luther's movement appealed to "devout persons who were shocked by abuses in the church, to the worldly who saw a chance to appropriate church lands and riches for themselves, to patriots who wanted to nationalize the church, and to princes and nobles who were eager to increase their political power, as well as to those university professors and students who were impressed by Luther's theological arguments." [53]

To this movement Luther gave untiring energy and leadership. So did his devoted follower, Philip Melanchthon. As a result, princes, burghers, clergymen and peasants rose against the Church in Germany, seized its property and abolished the traditional forms of worship. The peasants, downtrodden victims of a harsh social and economic system, were particularly aroused by Luther's ideas on Christian liberty and translated them to fit their economic oppression as well as their subservience to the Roman Church. Spurred on by fanatical leaders like Thomas Munzer, the peasants at first made what would represent to us in the twentieth century quite moderate demands. They were all refused. The peasants then rose in open revolt in 1524 against lay lords as well as the Church. Shocked by the excesses of the rough peasantry, Luther threw his support to the nobles, urging them to strike down the peasant hordes, and "remember that nothing can be more poisonous, harmful, or devilish than a man in rebellion." [54]

The revolt was crushed in blood and over fifty thousand peasants were killed. Not only was the lot of the peasant class worsened as a result of rebellion but Luther's influence was repudiated in most of south Germany, which was ready to be reconciled to Rome.

The princes of Germany were now divided into a Catholic and a Lutheran party. When the Catholic Emperor, Charles V, ordered that all the laws against heretics be enforced the Lutherans protested and were known thereafter as *Protestants*. There were efforts made to unify the two religious factions in Germany under a moderate statement of the new teachings but the Diet refused to recognize the Lutheran creed. In 1531 the Lutheran princes formed a League at Schmalkald and fought against the imperial forces until 1555, when the Truce of Augsburg provided that each prince could choose the religion of his subjects.

The triumph of Lutheranism was not limited to Germany. In Sweden (now independent of Denmark) the ruler Gustavus Vasa (1523-1560) used laws, propaganda and force to convert his country to the new religion. Frederick I of Denmark and Norway also saw the possibility of increasing his political control by adopting Lutheranism. By the end of the century the Scandinavian countries were firmly Lutheran.

There was a religious revolt in Switzerland, begun by a Catholic priest, Ulrich Zwingli, who believed also in a priesthood of the true believer and in individual interpretation of Scripture. When Zwingli was killed in the religious civil war, a French refugee-reformer came to Geneva and soon was preaching a doctrine that would, in the generation after Luther, sweep a great part of France, the Low Countries, and Scotland away from the Catholic Church. Calvinism was "a militant, crusading religion that had eliminated all the softness and indulgence from Lutheranism." [55] The keen, logical mind of John Calvin (1509-64) developed the doctrine that God foreordains those who are to be saved and those who are to be damned. This is predestination. Calvinism also repudiated state patronage of religion. In Geneva, Calvin established a theocracy, in which the state was merely an arm of the

Church or a Church-state where the Calvinist ministers ruled and judged and punished all the sins of men. Calvin established a great college where the Calvinist ministers were trained—many of them ex-priests and religious, whose labors won thousands of converts to Calvin's teachings.

A third area of religious upheaval was England where King Henry VIII despaired of having a son by his first wife, Catherine of Aragon, whose daughter, Mary, was heir to the English throne. Capitalizing on the technicality of a papal dispensation which had made his marriage lawful in the Church (Catherine had been the bride of Henry's brother, Arthur, for a few months before his death), Henry wanted Pope Clement VII (1523-34) to revoke this dispensation originally granted by an earlier Pope, Julius II, and declare his marriage to Catherine annulled. Aside from the sophistry in his proposition, for Henry had been married to Catherine for sixteen years and she had borne him eight children (only one of whom survived), the Pope was in no position to rule out a decision of an earlier Pope. Moreover, Pope Clement could hardly rule in favor of Henry and against Catherine, for the Holy Roman Emperor, Charles V, was her nephew, ready with troops to avenge his outraged aunt.

When Henry came to realize that in Rome's eyes his marriage was valid he was left only two alternatives: submission to the Pope's decision or repudiation of the papal primacy over the universal Church. He chose the latter course—and even had himself declared the supreme head on earth of the Church of Christ, so far as England was concerned. Subjects refusing to swear an oath acknowledging this were sentenced to death. Thus it was that "a gallant minority," including Carthusians, other monks, a few secular priests, the Bishop of Rochester (John Fisher) and Sir Thomas More, went to the scaffold rather than renounce their faith.

Upon the basis of advice and investigations carried out by his Chancellor, Thomas Cromwell, Henry VIII dissolved England's monasteries, broke up the chantries, confiscated their wealth and parceled it out among his loyal middle-class supporters. It should be stressed, however, that Henry only established a schismatic Church, and did not change Catholic doctrines. During the minority of Henry's sickly son, Edward VI (1547-53), the Calvinistic party gained the upper hand as the boy King's counselors and regents. Mass was now forbidden and a Protestant rite substituted.

Mary succeeded Edward. A proud Catholic, and a true daughter of her humiliated Spanish mother, Mary (1553-58) restored Catholicism to all but the confiscated monasteries in England. The papal legate, Cardinal Reginald Pole, on the Queen's invitation, absolved England before a joint session of Parliament of the sin of schism and rejoined the island to union with Rome. All bishops who had earlier renounced Rome were now deprived of office. But the Marian restoration was only temporary. Mary was married to the great champion of Catholicism, Philip II of Spain. When the childless queen, who went down in history as "Bloody Mary" for the vigorous persecution of heresy during her short reign, died, and was succeeded by Elizabeth, daughter of Henry and Ann Boleyn, the Protestant regime, part Calvinist, part Lutheran, of Edward VI was again set up. Now it came about that to say or hear Mass or even be a priest in England would entail death.

What Luther, Calvin, Zwingli and John Knox did was not reform the Catholic Church in which they were all baptized but to build up new systems based on their own revolutionary theological doctrines. But the Catholic Church did not disappear. The loss of many millions of its faithful weakened it, and limited it, but did not destroy it. Within the Church, the movement to root out abuses, to tighten up administration, to overhaul the whole mechanism, a movement which had never wholly ceased, even under the worst Popes, was renewed now, as the great structure of Christian unity was buffeted by the storms of controversy and shattered on the rocks of heresy and schism. The movement for reform had been unduly delayed and obstructed from gaining momentum until after the worst damage was irretrievably done. But in spite of these setbacks, the Catholic Church of the sixteenth century finally underwent a reform "in head and members" and ultimately surrendered nothing of its age-old doctrine though storms of controversy continued to rage about St. Peter's frail bark.

XXIII

The Catholic Reformation

As history records, reform of the Catholic Church was long delayed. The evil practices of generations had produced a vested interest in the maintenance of abuses. Wherever reforming cardinals spoke out against the sale of offices, or the exorbitant fees for the sacraments, or the holding of multiple benefices, or the abuse of wide preaching of indulgences, apathy greeted them.

During his short but remarkable reign the Dutch Pope, Adrian VI (1522-23), sent a legate to prosecute the task of saving Germany for Catholicism; he was instructed to admit that the Lutheran heresy was a scourge due especially to the sins of the prelates and the clergy. But this simple confession, meant as an assurance of the Pope's real will to reform the Church, was only another testimonial to the truth of Lutheran propaganda. The Diet of Nuremberg, where the Catholic clergy held the majority of seats, refused to put the anti-Lutheran decrees into execution. The German higher clergy was as indifferent to the progress of Lutheranism as they had for generations been indifferent to the fortunes of Catholicism. This inertia was to be one of Rome's major difficulties for the next seventy years.[56]

In Catholic Italy, one would not look for the triumph of the Protestant creed; yet in Italy there were people who felt even more keenly than the Germans or the Swiss the need for reforming the abuses that were demoralizing the Church. Consequently, the Italian argument was all for reform within the Church. Certain bishops like Carafa led the way to reform by resigning all their benefices and distributing their substantial wealth among the poor.

More than some earlier epochs this was a period of great saints. They included St. Philip Neri (1515-95), a young Florentine nobleman who gathered twelve laymen together each Sunday after Mass and traveled to some basilica or rural green to hold pious talks and sing religious music. They became the Fathers of the Oratory of Divine Love and originated the oratorio. From his lonely office in the Vatican St. Philip directed the reform of the Roman curia, working simply, unostentatiously, building a new type of spiritually minded clerical official—a new race whence were to come nuncios, cardinals, legates and Popes. The new religious orders, such as the Oratory of the Divine Love and the Theatines (also founded in the early 1500's), had for their purpose "to make up what is wanting in the clergy . . . corrupted by vice and ignorance to the ruin of the people." Their members spread throughout Europe, and their example, combined with the Jesuits and Capuchins, helped to restore the moral fiber of the Catholic clergy and the Popes. These orders heralded the onset of reform in the ancient Church. The progress of the Reformation gave new urgency to the need and the demand.

St. Charles Borromeo (1538-84) was a nephew of Pius IV; Charles resigned his office as cardinal in Rome to cleanse the religious life of Milan. After he ordered religious societies to obey their rule, a group of discontented members of the order of the Umiliati fired a shot at him as he knelt praying in chapel. In 1610 Pope Paul V canonized one who thought reform the best answer to the Protestant revolt. His influence was felt throughout Italy and shared in transforming the cardinals from worldly aristocrats to devoted priests.

The most interesting figure in this era of monastic reform was the frail, masterful abbess, Teresa of Avila (1515-82), the great Spanish mystic responsible for the reform of her order and the founding of the discalced (shoeless) Carmelites, an order of nuns entirely shut off from the world. These sisters wore sandals of rope, slept on straw, ate no meat, and remained strictly within their convent. From Avila St. Teresa went on to Malaga, Segovia and Toledo, where she helped reform other orders of Carmelite priests and nuns.

Another agent in this great Spanish revival of the Carmelite order and the contemplative life was St. John of the Cross (1542-91). He too was born near Avila, where his father worked as a weaver. John went to school and worked in a hospital at Medina del Campo, where he entered the Carmelite order in 1563; the following year he was sent to the university at Salamanca. Shortly after his ordination in 1567 he met St. Teresa of Avila at Medina and she persuaded him to introduce her reform among the friars. Though he met with strong opposition and was twice kidnaped, and imprisoned for nine months in Toledo, where he wrote some of his poetry, he escaped and went on to found reformed communities in the south of Spain. In 1588 he went to Madrid to attend the first general chapter of the reformed friars, and was appointed prior of Segovia. Three years later he moved to Ubeda, where he died, December 14, 1591.

Renowned more for his writings than for his life, John of the Cross wrote a number of books, such as

The Ascent of Mount Carmel, which deals with the development of mystical experience in the soul. Though his output was small, he is regarded as one of the greatest lyrical poets of Spanish literature.

The eleven-year reign of Clement VII (1523-34) was one long disaster. As Giulano de Medici he had been an admirable bishop of Florence, but as Pope he was timorous and vacillating. This cousin of Leo X continued to act too much as an Italian priest and too little as a moral and religious leader of Catholicism in the contest which under him was joined with Zwinglians and Anglicans as well as Lutherans. The new Pope was soon at war with the Faith's one champion in Germany, the Emperor Charles V, and in 1527 an imperial army —half Lutheran and half Spanish—took Rome and sacked it with a barbarity rare even in those days. The Pope was for months the Emperor's prisoner.

Next a demand was made for a general council, but Clement feared it would result in a diminution of his power. Conciliarism could be revived, he feared, with devastating results. To meet the insistent demands of the Emperor, Clement agreed to a council on condition that the Protestants first return to their obedience and then agree to abide by the council's decisions. The Protestants, of course, refused. What Rome failed to recognize was that by now Protestantism was a vested interest, an organization, and not merely a matter of the erroneous views of German theologians.

With England lost to Rome and the communications with Germany wholly broken off, matters were in a most unsatisfactory condition when Clement died. Alessandro Farnese was unanimously elected to succeed him. "He was a frail old man of sixty-six, shattered in health but, as Titian's marvelous portraits bear witness, with nothing abated of his intellectual power or his natural fire." [57]

This first reforming Pope, Paul III (1534-49), was wise enough to realize that "our Holy Mother Church has been so changed . . . that no trace can be found in her of humility, temperance, continence and Apostolic strength." Once elected, he lost no time in appointing a committee of cardinals to draw up a program of moral renovation for the Church. He sent a series of wandering commissions to tour Germany and report on conditions there. This represents the foundation for the system of modern nuncios, through which the reforming Papacy was chiefly to act.

At his first consistory Pope Paul announced his decision to call the long desired council. The Bull of Summons appeared in 1536. The Protestants rebelled; once more their theologians declared war on Catholicism and their princes handed back unopened the invitations to the council. The French, at war with the Holy Roman Emperor, used the dangers of wartime travel as their excuse for absenting themselves from the council.

But Pope Paul was a determined man. He decided upon Mantua as the location for the meeting; however, four weeks before its opening the Duke of Mantua refused the hospitality of his city. Vicenza was the next choice, but there, in 1538, only five bishops appeared. The Pope apparently stood alone in his zeal for reform. At that point he was confronted with the difficult task of preventing a compromise between the Lutherans and the Holy Roman Emperor on doctrinal differences.

The Council finally came together in December, 1545, not at Mantua or Vicenza but at Trent, an imperial city beyond the Italian frontier in the Tyrol.

Trent was chosen largely because of its location between German-speaking and Italian-speaking people. The Pope's Council came about as a result of his patience, diplomatic skill and determination to reform the Church.

Difficulties had postponed the convocation and further difficulties repeatedly interrupted its labors. Nevertheless the Council of Trent effected a great reform in the Church and preserved intact Catholic doctrine. The Catholic bishops at Trent made no doctrinal changes and offered no compromises to the Protestants. They merely confirmed the main points in Catholic theology as expounded by Thomas Aquinas in the thirteenth century. The Bible and historic tradition form the basis of the Christian religion and the interpretation of Holy Scripture belongs to the Church. Protestant teachings about grace and justification by faith were condemned.

The Emperor had wanted a council chiefly to reform abuses. He feared the results of clear definitions on doctrinal points in dispute between Catholics and Protestants. The Pope, however, insisted on the dogmatic work of the Council. Commissions of experts drafted the decrees, which were discussed in private sessions and then, when a decision was reached, it was solemnly promulgated in a public session. Once Catholic doctrine was clearly reaffirmed there could be no hope of reconciliation between Catholic and Protestant theory.

Meanwhile one of the ablest of Sacred Colleges was being created by Pope Paul III. While official Rome made merry, the new cardinals worked and in March, 1537, they presented their now-famous report, *The Advice of the Commission of the Cardinals on the Reform of the Church Set Forth at the Command of Pope Paul III.* Here was virtually embodied the whole of the reform that Trent was later to enact. The Pope did not wait for the Council to meet before undertaking the general work of reforming the clergy. Hundreds of Pope Paul's directives have been found for the reform of monasteries and convents in every part of Europe.

The plague broke out in Trent and the Pope acquiesced when a majority of the Council voted to withdraw to Bologna. Ten days later, Charles V gained the greatest military victory of his career over the Protestants at Muhlberg. This put him in an extremely strong position and he forced the suspension of the Council in 1548.

Julius III (1550-55), who had been Giammaria Cardinal del Monte, and the first president of the Council of Trent, succeeded Pope Paul III and in 1551 he reconvened the Council of Trent. Work went on admirably and a whole series of disciplinary statutes was enacted, both by this and by the subsequent session of 1562. The sale of Church offices was forbidden; bishops and other prelates were forced to live in their dioceses, abandon worldly pursuits and devote their time to spiritual labors. Seminaries were to be established for the education and training of priests. Sermons were to be preached in the vernacular rather than in Latin; indulgences were not to be dispensed for money and plural offices were forbidden.

The movement for internal reform was accelerated when Cardinal Giovanni Pietro Carafa was elected Pope as Paul IV (1555-59). Through him at last the paganism of the Renaissance was driven from the Papacy. He dismissed his licentious secretary, Cardinal Carlo Carafa, in 1559 and banished two other nephews who had disgraced the pontificate. Nepotism, which had flourished there for a century, was driven from the Vatican. Bishops, monks or abbots not serving in some official capacity in Rome were required to return to their monasteries or dioceses under pain of suspension. All departments of the Church were ordered to reduce their fees and eliminate any suspicion of the sale of offices or articles. The Papacy itself ended the customary payments for high appointments. Over outcries from the Roman aristocrats, severe papal edicts were issued against usurers, actors and prostitutes. During the ensuing years the Council of Trent produced decrees on other Church teachings; this mass of reformatory and dogmatic legislation was to set the pattern of Catholic life for the next three hundred years.

The central government of the Church was also reorganized. A uniform catechism was prepared and a standard edition of the Bible, the so called Latin Vulgate or Saint Jerome's translation, was adopted. A list called the *Index* was prepared of dangerous and heretical books which Catholics were prohibited from reading. By all these efforts, discipline was restored, morals purified and the scandal of clerical worldliness restrained. Lapses from these strict laws of faith and conduct were to be punished by the medieval court of the Inquisition, which now redoubled its activity, especially in Italy and Spain.

Pius IV died in 1565, leaving to the Church as his legacy the completion of the sessions of the Council of Trent and a peaceful understanding with the Catholic powers. His successor was the one Pope of that era to be canonized, Michele Ghislieri, a Dominican monk, who took the name of Pius V (1566-72). To this saintly, and at the same time vigorous, man fell the task of inaugurating the practical application of the new reform legislation. He made obedience to the decrees of Trent the one rule of his life.

His two immediate successors, Gregory XIII (1572-

85) and Sixtus V (1585-90), are the Popes who began the offensive against the successful heresies. They, too, dedicated themselves to a vigorous enforcement of the decrees of the Council of Trent. Not only did they found numerous colleges and seminaries for the education of the clergy, but they also entered the field of national and international politics, attempting, through the instrument of the new diplomatic service they created, to form combinations of Catholic princes for the defeat of the Protestants and the extirpation of heresy.

It was Pope Pius V who excommunicated and deposed Elizabeth of England. Gregory XIII sent an army against her into Ireland, and continued to work against her on the continent until the end of his reign. Sixtus V subsidized the Spanish Armada. So we see that wherever there was hope of an offensive against the newly established Protestant regimes, these Popes stood ready to supply money, if not arms.

Their most enduring work, however, was the reformation of Catholic life and the constructive application of the decrees of Trent, and their chief auxiliaries were the new religious orders.[58] These orders, which were formed to deepen the spiritual life of the people and to support the Church in its reforming efforts, were a very important factor in the Catholic revival, not only in preserving all Southern Europe for the Church but also in preventing the complete triumph of Protestantism in the north.

The Franciscan reform produced the Capuchins, who provided the Popes of the next hundred and fifty years with an array of zealous, well-trained, popular preachers who had a large share in the victories of the Counter Reformation in Germany, Italy and France. The new order—the Theatines, founded in 1524 by Giovanni Pietro Carafa (1476-1559) and St. Cajetan (1480-

1547), were priests living under the three vows of poverty, chastity and obedience but doing the work of the secular clergy. Their vow of poverty was especially rigorous; they were not even allowed to beg. They were given encouragement by the Pope and supplied him with priests to reform the long neglected dioceses of Italy. Pope Paul III also encouraged and blessed the great work of the first Ursuline nuns.

The most celebrated of all these orders, both for its sixteenth-century labors and for its subsequent history, was the one approved by Pope Paul III in 1540. This was the Society of Jesus, whose members are known as Jesuits. This order was founded in 1534 by a Spanish nobleman and soldier, Ignatius Loyola. His was not only a new order but a new kind of order. The discipline was novel in its military strictness. There was a long novitiate and training period during which authority and obedience were stressed. At the end of this education four vows were taken—the usual three and a fourth vow of special allegiance to the Pope. St. Ignatius Loyola's *Spiritual Exercises* produced the most perfectly subordinated instrument the Papacy has ever had at its disposal. Wherever the Holy See needed them, the Jesuits went—and wherever they went, they established an enviable reputation as preachers, controversialists, teachers and confessors. Appreciating that the Church of that age was confronted with conditions of war rather than of peace, the Jesuits did not content themselves with prayer and works of peace, with charity and local benevolence, but adapted themselves to the new circumstances and endeavored in many ways to restore all things to the Catholic Church. They rushed to the front in the religious conflict; they sought to educate the young, and as educators they had no equals in Europe. Such a scholar as Francis Bacon testified of Jesuit teaching that "nothing better has been put in practice." By their learning, no less than by the purity of their lives, they restored respect for the Catholic clergy.

Perhaps the role of the Society and its influence has been exaggerated; it has certainly been controversial. But in the records of their first great saints, Ignatius Loyola, Francis Xavier, Francis Borgia, Peter Canisius, Aloysius Gonzaga and Robert Bellarmine, is written the whole history of this one side of the Counter Reformation. St. Peter Canisius, the first German Jesuit, was to Germany a second Boniface, and St. Robert Bellarmine gave a direction to Catholic theological life which it followed for another two centuries. Jesuits were responsible for the recovery of Poland after it seemed lost to Calvinism. They similarly preserved the Faith in Bavaria and the southern Netherlands. Risking their very lives, they ministered daily to fellow Catholics in Elizabethan England. In their missionary work in India, China, among the Indians of North America and among the aborigines of Brazil and Paraguay, they utilized politics, agriculture, literature and science.

The Society of Jesus was one of the mightiest opponents of the new nationalism. The views of the great Jesuit writers on political science, like Suarez and Robert Bellarmine, were disapproved even by Catholic princes. Because of the teaching of Suarez, the Jesuits were accused of advocating regicide. One of their writers, Mariana, was even repudiated by the Society itself, for advocating the assassination of tyrants who could not otherwise be removed. At the end of the sixteenth century, the Jesuit Superior General, Aquaviva, denied the Society advocated regicide and enacted grave penalties against any who argued that interference in politics, which was legitimate, might go to the lengths of assassination. Jesuit difficulties stemmed mainly from their strong antinationalism. Many Catholic pamphlets of this period denounced them. The final tragedy after all their great triumphs—and the proof of the shackles the lay princes would put on the Church—was Pope Clement XIV's enforced suppression of the Jesuits in 1773. Regalism secured their suppression; the Papacy can be defended only on the plea that the part must be sacrificed to save the whole.

If economic and political conditions were favorable to the rapid diffusion of Protestantism, then it must be added with equal truth that political and economic causes co-operated with religious developments to maintain the supremacy of the Catholic Church in at least half of the countries of Europe where it had dominated in 1500.

XXIV

The New World

As the great geographic discoveries of the fifteenth and sixteenth century opened a New World to European civilization, Christian missionaries went forth to win new souls for the Church. In this New World, born in the years after Columbus sailed westward, the Roman Catholic Church established "a beachhead" wherever explorers or colonists went in the Western Hemisphere. The beginnings of a world-wide mission that would unfold with the nineteenth century were made. In its mission work the Church entered territories never before Christianized, such as the vacuum it met in American Indian country. In size and in wealth these new world Catholic districts far exceeded those in Europe.

Now the Papacy found itself occupied with a whole world. It was therefore forced to confine its activity to matters mainly religious. This change in papal outlook was completed with the establishment of the mission in the Americas, where the Church began to advance. Now papal attention had to be directed to the world-wide problems of the universal Church. "The torn and stormed Rome of the sixteenth century was learning to realize anew the essential missionary character of the faith." [59] Wherever explorers and exploiters went, there were Jesuits, Dominicans or members of other orders, prevailing upon shipowners, giving their lives for the cause they advocated. The Church was learning from

189

explorers; it was profiting from the prodding of reformed Christians. The immediate expression of its new
health was the desire for expansion.

While the great voyages of discovery were intended
to open rich Oriental trade routes, acquire wealth and
political power, the expansion of Christianity was also
their goal. It is one of the ironic facts of history that
just when so many European countries were separating
from Rome in the sixteenth century, the Church was on
the brink of Christianizing wide regions of the New
World with great future possibilities.

In the course of time four European countries gained
possessions in America: Spain, Portugal, England and
France. Spain appeared on the scene before the other
powers. She eventually carved out an empire branching
out from Mexico, Central America and the West Indies
(New Spain), on the North American Continent into
Texas, Florida and up the coast of California. Juan
Ponce de Leon, a former Governor of Puerto Rico, first
planted the Spanish flag in Florida. He sailed along the
east and west coasts in 1513 and a few years later he
made an unsuccessful attempt to plant a colony on the
western coast. It was the Easter season when he first
saw the new land, and so he called it Florida (*pascua
Florida* being the Spanish phrase for Easter Sunday).
His successor, Vasquez de Ayllon, set out from Haiti
in 1526, with six hundred colonists and a Dominican
friar for the coast of Virginia, where they made a settlement near Jamestown, eighty years before the English
arrived there. However, pestilence killed half the settlers
and drove the rest back to Haiti.

On another expedition Francisco Vasquez de Coro-
nado took two hundred seventy men, including six
Franciscans, through regions of Arizona and New
Mexico in search of the famed "Seven Cities of Cibola,"

rumored to contain gold and silver in abundance. The Spaniards were sorely disappointed to find nothing but a few Zuñi pueblos. Coronado kept going farther north, still in search of gold, and explored central Kansas. When the expedition returned to Mexico City, two of the Franciscans remained in New Mexico; nothing was ever heard from them. A third friar went on toward southwestern Kansas where hostile Indians murdered him.

The Spanish established their first permanent settlement in Florida in 1565, when Pedro Menéndez de Avilés, colonizer and naval genius, landed with 1500 soldiers and colonists at a harbor he called San Augustin, the present St. Augustine, oldest city in the United States. That same year Father Mendoza founded his mission there, the first parish in the United States. The second region colonized by the Spanish was New Mexico under Don Juan de Oñate (1598). With ten Franciscans in his party he set up a settlement with its capital at Santa Fe. Here a parish church was built in 1662 and twenty years later the friars could boast of having about sixty thousand baptized Indians in the region. Much later, the Spanish occupied the territory of Texas, where the Franciscan friar, Massenet, laid the plans for the foundation of some twenty-five permanent missions.

In the Spanish empire carved out by the Conquistadores, the work of the humble monks who taught the Indians Catholic Christianity was in shining contrast to the brutality of the military leaders. Both by precept and by example the monks presented Christianity as a religion of love and selfless service. Many of them sealed their testimony with their life's blood. To the uneducated native this new religion must have offered bewildering contrasts. "Spanish" and "Christian" were identical in the Indian's mind, and both were equally odious. No wonder the Indian spirit of vengeance sometimes found an outlet in the killing of their real friend, the missionary. Bartolomé de Las Casas, who had arrived in the New World as Columbus' secretary in 1498, and who witnessed the succession of massacres led by Panfilo de Narvaez, which all but wiped out the native inhabitants of Cuba, returned to Spain in 1547 to plead the Indians' cause. After pouring out a stream of protest in books, letters and speeches, he received the support of Cardinal Ximenes. Thereafter the Spanish government formulated the new laws of 1542 which protected the Indians and saved them from extinction, but these laws were very difficult to enforce from Spain.

In the New World a group of Franciscans carried Spanish colonization to the shores of the Pacific and built a village which was to grow into San Francisco. Christianity thus came to what is now California largely through them and the efforts of Father Junipero Serra. The Jesuits had labored in this region prior to 1767 but they were unable to continue their activities because in 1767 King Charles III issued his edict expelling them from Spain and the Spanish possessions. The Franciscans were sent by the King to replace the Jesuits. Father Serra and a group of missioners arrived in Mexico in 1749 and he insisted on walking the 250 miles from Vera Cruz to Mexico City because, he said, St. Francis had never given his monks the permission to ride. On the way he suffered a snake bite that left him lame. In 1769 Serra went north from Mexico with Governor Portola and founded the mission at San Diego, thus beginning that remarkable chain of missions he established along the California coast extending from San Diego to Sonoma, a distance of about six hundred miles. Making his headquarters at Monterey, the praesidio, he built at nearby Carmel the mission church dedicated to St. Charles Borromeo, before whose altar Father Serra now lies buried. Up and down *el camino real,* a mere footpath then, went Father Serra and his Franciscans from mission to mission, and all along the way he was greeted by the three words with which he habitually opened his instruction periods: *"Amar a Dios"* (Love God). A familiar sight to all was Father Serra on his half-crippled legs, baptizing and confirming thousands (because of a shortage of bishops, Pope Clement XIV granted him that privilege in 1774), and founding missions whose names sound like songs: San Juan Capistrano, San Gabriel, San Francisco, San Luis Obispo, San Buenaventura, San Luis Rey, Santa Clara and San Antonio de Padua[60]—the names of saints beloved of the Spanish pioneers. This is not a complete list, and many of the missions were founded after Serra's death in 1784, when his work was continued by Fr. Fermin de Lasuen, who added nine missions to "Serra's Rosary" and ran them at their apogee. Included among them was Santa Barbara, "Queen of the Missions."

The missions were more than mere churches—they were small islands of civilization—real communities in a desert of sand and ignorance. The missionaries, who were paid a fixed salary by the government, performed a truly remarkable task, for the California Indians were of a backward, degraded sort and so stubborn that the friars sometimes labored years to make a single convert. Besides the church (many of the church sanctuaries and walls still display the designs and ornamentation painted by the natives with vegetable dyes), each mission had a school where farming and manual training were taught. Guest rooms were available for travelers. The monks saw to it that the

people were provided with plenty of harmless amuse-
ment. The Indians were taught the Spanish dances and
nearly every station had an orchestra. Everywhere the
system was the same. A small garrison, subject to the
padres, was maintained; their main function was to keep
order. The lands and buildings of the missions belonged
to the converts themselves.[61]

The prosperity of the missions was one cause of their
downfall. A vast amount of grain was raised on their
farmlands and at one period there were nearly a quarter
of a million head of cattle, even more sheep, and thousands of mules, horses, hogs and goats. This wealth,
owned in common by the natives, with the friars acting
as administrators, was coveted by the troubled Mexican
government and Mexican politicians who cast avaricious
eyes toward California after throwing off Spanish rule.
Salaried commissioners were appointed by the Mexican
government and in 1834, by one subterfuge or another,
half the mission lands passed immediately into private
hands, and the other half was soon lost to landsharks.
The friars were expelled and secular priests who had
little opportunity to do much for the development of
the Indians, were sent to replace them.

When the Mexican War broke out with the United
States in 1846, the Indians became almost hopelessly
degenerated, the churches began to fall into ruin,
and hardly any vestige remained of the Franciscan
mission system. What had been built up in sixty years
was destroyed almost at a blow. Yet, while in California, the Franciscans are said to have baptized more
than a hundred thousand souls. According to one
report, the Spaniards in Mexico alone seem to have
baptized over nine millions from 1536 to 1540. Though
the Indians and the padres were to pass from the scene,
California had a glorious missionary history until the

secularization effected in 1835. With the acquisition by the United States of this Mexican territory, the work of Catholic revival had largely to begin all over again, but it was put upon a better basis. As a result of a long suit before the United States Land Commission, the Church was awarded large tracts of land formerly belonging to the missions. Had it not been for the annexation of California by the United States, the Church there would have been robbed without any hope of redress.

In the aftermath of American conquest and accession, a Catholic revival began. Gradually the Church became non-Spanish in character and took on the status of a minority group, but growth was real and sustained. There was a magnificent foundation on which to build.[62]

The French entered American territories to the north and west of the English settlements and balanced the Spanish southern thrust. In Canada, around the Great Lakes, along the St. Lawrence and down the Mississippi, settlements were made. There another story of splendid accomplishments and heroic efforts unfolded.

After establishing Quebec in 1608, the governor of New France, Samuel de Champlain, invited the Franciscan Recollects to come as missionaries to Canada, and they were soon joined by Sulpicians who came to Montreal, and French Jesuits, who enjoyed the greatest success in the evangelization of Canada. About 1639, the first Ursuline nuns came to Quebec from Tours under the leadership of the Venerable Marie de l'Incarnation. With them came a group of nursing sisters of Notre Dame, who established the first hospital in Canada.

In 1659, François de Montmorency Laval arrived with the powers of Vicar Apostolic and the see of this first bishop of Canada was established at Quebec in 1674. It remained until near the end of the eighteenth century the only episcopal see in North America and had jurisdiction over the vast French province stretching from Hudson's Bay to Louisiana. About fifty dioceses were eventually created out of this former French territory. Laval built a seminary and established a number of parishes outside the city. A great and capable churchman, Bishop Laval fought for the welfare of the Indians and organized a splendid educational system.

The Jesuit Fathers, John Brébeuf and Gabriel Lalemand, came to Canada in 1625. Within a few years other Jesuits joined them. From Quebec, the saintly Father Jacques Marquette started out on his labors among the Indians on the shores of Lake Superior. Later, in 1673, he reached the Mississippi River and explored its valley with the Franciscan, Louis Hennepin, and the adventurer, Louis Joliet, thus establishing beyond all question that the river flowed into the Gulf of Mexico. Of exploration in this northern region, Frederic Bancroft wrote: "Not a cape was turned, or a river entered, but a Jesuit led the way." Though the sons of Ignatius Loyola were primarily missionaries, not explorers, it was from their pens—writing in canoes or in the depths of the forests or in smoky wigwams— that we get our greatest wealth of geographical and ethnographical knowledge of the French empire in America. It is to the seventy-three published volumes of the *Jesuit Relations* that every historian of the period must go.[63]

The Jesuits were responsible for many of the missions in the Lakes region. Some ventured into what is now Maine. Fathers Dablon and Marquette helped establish a mission at Sault Sainte Marie. Other Jesuits carried the Gospel to the western shore of Lake Huron and south of Lake Ontario after 1660. Here was the home of the saintly Indian, Kateri Tekawitha, "the Lily of the Mohawks," who died in 1680. Her bones are preserved near Montreal in the Church of an Indian village, where the people still sing the responses to the Mass in Iroquois.

The most famous of the missionaries was Father Isaac Jogues, a courageous French Jesuit who labored among the savage Iroquois Indians. We know the dramatic story of how he was captured and tortured by the Iroquois, escaped, was smuggled on board a Dutch ship and taken to France. Pope Urban VIII gave him special permission to say Mass despite his mangled hands, with these words: "It would be shameful that a martyr of Christ should not be allowed to drink the Blood of Christ." Jogues eagerly returned to the missions. This time there was no torture, but the sudden blow of a tomahawk. His martyrdom at Auriesville made him the first North American saint, canonized in 1930. St. Réné Goupil, a Jesuit lay brother, also met death at the same place in 1642.

In 1682 Robert Cavalier de La Salle followed the Mississippi River to the Gulf of Mexico. It was Father Membré, one of his companions, who said the first Mass in Louisiana. More Ursuline nuns came from France to New Orleans, where they established the first Catholic academy in what is now the United States (1727).

Great good was accomplished by these heroic priests and sisters; despite Indian uprisings in which many were killed and their missions destroyed. The work of the French missionaries in the early seventeenth century does not appear as tremendous a success as does the work of the Spanish missionaries in North and South America. But we must remember that the Frenchman did not receive the same wholehearted support from the Crown as did the Spaniard. Moreover, they had to cope with hostile English Protestants to the south and grasping French traders who wanted neither an increase in the population nor too many civilized Indians. "The Black robes of New France counted their conversions by hundreds, or at best by thousands; those of New Spain, working in a more propitious vineyard, numbered their baptisms by hundreds of thousands, or even by millions. . . . The imposing stature of the Jesuits of New France is widely known because they had [Francis] Parkman as their historian. The Spanish Jesuits in North America await their Parkman." [64]

Though England controlled much less territory in the New World than France or Spain, her colonies had a more lasting influence on developments there. Until after the American Revolution, the colony of Pennsylvania, which was originally a Quaker settlement, provided the only permanent haven for Catholics. At intervals the colonies of Maryland and Rhode Island permitted Catholics to worship lawfully.

The first group of Catholic colonists came to Maryland in 1634. Sir George Calvert, who was a close friend of King James I, planned a colonizing venture in the New World as a place of refuge for the persecuted of all religions. In 1625, Calvert was converted to Catholicism, which necessitated his resignation as Secretary of State. King James I, while accepting the resignation, elevated his friend to an Irish peerage as Baron of Baltimore, and continued to further his colonization schemes. An effort was made to plant a colony at a place called Avalon in Newfoundland, but it was abandoned. In search of a better climate, George Calvert, Lord Baltimore's son, sailed southward, reaching Jamestown in 1629. When he saw the Chesapeake Bay region, he determined upon it as the location for the new settlement. Returning to England to secure a charter, he left his wife and children behind him. A little later, they perished at sea following him back to England. This may partially account for his untimely death at the age of fifty-two. Before dying, however, he obtained the charter for Maryland from King Charles I. The colony was named for his Queen, Henrietta Maria. The charter was inherited by his son, Cecil Calvert, in 1632.

Catholics constituted only a minor part of the first group of settlers who crossed the ocean on the *Ark* and the *Dove*. An exclusively Catholic colony was never in the Baron's mind. Had he attempted one, the English authorities would have forbidden it. Yet the Catholics of early Maryland were an influential minority. The Jesuit Father, Andrew White, celebrated the first Mass in English North America on the party's arrival at St. Mary's in 1634, and later wrote an interesting account of the voyage.

The first governor of Maryland was Leonard Calvert, brother of Cecil. The patent gave Lord Baltimore and his heirs a vast extent of territory enclosing the northern half of Chesapeake Bay. As it happened, Baltimore's lands fell within the limits of the Virginia Company under its charter of 1609 and loud protests were heard, but the Virginians had to acquiesce in this infringement on their lands.

The provisions relating to religion in the Maryland charter were deliberately left vague. It merely indicated that the laws of the colony were to conform to the ecclesiastical laws of England. There was nothing to prevent the establishment of Catholic and dissenting churches. It is to the credit of Cecil Calvert and his successors that they used their authority in the interest of religious toleration. Their wise religious policy was embodied in the Toleration Act of 1649, which provided that no one professing belief in Christ should be in "any waies troubled, molested or discountenanced for or in respect of his or her religion, nor in the free exercise thereof." [65] Thus Maryland enjoys the distinction of being the first English colony where religious freedom was part of the common law.

About half the colonial Catholic population lived in Maryland and a quarter lived in Pennsylvania. Prior to the American Revolution, Catholics in the British colonies were under the direction of the Bishop of London. Bishop Challoner was the English superior of the American missions. In 1756, he wrote that there were twelve missionaries in Maryland and five in Pennsylvania and these priests secretly ministered to Catholics in New Jersey and Virginia.

Until 1773 the Jesuits ministered to the Catholics in Maryland. After their suppression the legal corporation of the Roman Catholic clergy continued to carry on mission work. Father John Lewis was their superior. In 1784 Father John Carroll, a native of Maryland, was appointed Prefect-Apostolic in the United States. Five years later he became the first Bishop of Baltimore, with the entire confederation of American states and all American territories as his diocese. One of the first labors of the new Bishop was the founding of Georgetown College (1789). To build up an American priesthood, Bishop Carroll brought a group of Sulpician Fathers from France who established St. Mary's Seminary at Baltimore (1791).

There were 25 priests and 30,000 Catholics in the United States in 1790. By 1800 there were 52 priests and 100,000 Catholics. In all Catholic Church history there is hardly any parallel to the rapid growth of the Church in the Americas.

XXV

Mission Fields of Asia and Africa

The geographic discoveries of the sixteenth century had opened a New World to European civilization and Christian missionary activity was winning new souls to the Church in this Western world. While members of religious orders labored here, their brethren among the Franciscans, Jesuits, Dominicans and later the Maryknollers and Redemptorists were attempting a still more arduous task in the East. Their objectives were the three major countries of the Far East: India, China and Japan.

The conversion of major parts of the Far East was due very largely to the labors of one man—St. Francis Xavier (1506-52), one of the first companions of St. Ignatius Loyola and one of the brightest spirits among the Jesuits. St. Francis has since been made the patron saint of the missions.

The beginnings of Christianity in India are clouded in uncertainty. When the Portuguese made their first settlement there at the opening of the sixteenth century they found a small group of scattered Christians. The work of the Franciscan missionaries is the first of which we have any definite knowledge. They accompanied Cabral to India in 1500 and labored with little success in Goa until the arrival of St. Francis Xavier in 1542. Here he collected the Portuguese children for prayer and instruction. Before long thousands of natives came from neighboring towns to hear him. At times St. Francis put his instructions into writing for the more intelligent.

After laboring in India for three years, St. Francis traveled to the Portuguese colonies of Malaya, Malacca and the Moluccas, where he used these same techniques developed in India with such success. In 1549 he went to Japan, where the dangers were greater. When he left, two years later, he had impressed the highest ranks of society and converted nearly three thousand Japanese. Thirty years later there were over 200,000 converts and 250 churches in Japan. Meanwhile, Xavier was planning to enter China, the wealthiest, most populated and influential country in the East. However, he died of tropical fever on a small Pacific island called Sancian in 1552 at the age of forty-six before he could realize his ambition to bring Christ to nearby China.

Wherever he had preached during his lifetime the Catholic Faith continued to prosper. His work in Japan was followed by the establishment of a great Christian Church there, but the hostility of the state gathered momentum until 1587 when it burst forth in persecution which recalled the days of violence under the Roman empire. St. Philip of Jesus (1571-97) was a Franciscan missionary trained in the Philippines. When he set sail for mission work in Mexico (1596), a storm blew his ship off course to Japan, then ruled by the viciously anti-Christian Hideyoshi. The discovery of cannon and ammunition aboard his ship created suspicions of a plot to conquer the country.

The enraged Emperor ordered all missionaries to leave the country within two weeks and he ordered the arrest of Philip and the other Franciscans in Kyoto. In the days that followed, more Catholics were arrested. The prisoners, their ears cropped, were paraded through the streets of Kyoto and Osaka. On February 5, 1597, they were brought to Nagasaki. The group included six Franciscan missioners, three Japanese Jesuits and seventeen lay Christians. One of these was a thirteen-year-old boy, St. Thomas Kosaki. On his last night in prison, the Japanese boy had written his mother that he would see her in heaven.

The martyrs faced death bravely—even joyfully. The Japanese authorities had ordered them to be crucified. On their crosses, they sang hymns until the soldiers pierced their hearts with spears. The blood of these first twenty-six martyrs watered the seeds of Christianity planted in Japan by St. Francis Xavier half a century earlier.[66]

During an interval of peace which followed, more missionaries arrived in Japan, including Jesuits, Franciscans, Augustinians, Dominicans and, after 1609, some Protestants. A year later the persecutions were renewed. In 1622 Nagasaki was once again the gruesome scene of fifty-two executions on the same day. Fifteen years later over three thousand Catholics had been martyred for their faith and in 1640 Japan shut herself off from all foreign contacts of any kind. A handful of Japanese managed without priests or sacraments (except baptism) to cling to their Faith. Then came a marvelous revelation.

Missionaries had been admitted to the open ports of Japan after 1858 to serve the churches established for foreign residents. In 1865 a band of fifteen Japanese made known to missionaries that they were Catholics. Several thousand others were found still practicing the Faith they had kept alive for over two hundred years. This marked the beginning of Catholicism in modern Japan, where today there are 104,000 Catholics, several bishops and over one hundred native priests.

The great Jesuit missionary and astronomer, Father Matteo Ricci, did the first successful missionary work in China. Father Ricci adopted the methods used successfully by Xavier in Japan. He tried to win over the scholarly mandarins first, and then the great masses of the Chinese people. He therefore dressed as a mandarin and earned their respect through his scientific knowledge. He allowed prospective Chinese converts to keep all elements of their native culture that were not openly idolatrous or superstitious. This was to cause serious difficulty in the future.

Everyone is familiar with the story of how missionary priests penetrated into the very heart of Chinese culture, of their winning over the governing class, of their friendly relations with the emperors at Peking, of their rank at court as respected astronomers and their propaganda for the Faith. The Jesuits were the only missioners in China until 1631. After them came Franciscans and Dominicans and from the end of the seventeenth century Louis XIV began to send out priests from the newly founded seminary of the Missions Étrangères at Paris. The Lazarists or Vincentians also began to take a share in the work, and after the suppression of the Jesuits the Vincentian Fathers replaced them.

The mission in China, however, was not without difficulties. The Dominicans were shocked to find the Chinese using rites that seemed idolatrous. The matter was referred to Rome and the dispute continued until 1704, when Pope Clement XI prohibited the use of Chinese rites and all Chinese terms for God except

Tien-chu. In 1715 all concerned with Chinese missionary work were required to take an oath of obedience to the prohibition. The Jesuits and others obeyed but many of the native clergy apostasized, and the Chinese Emperor declared that he would not tolerate a religion which ran counter to all native customs. Persecutions broke out in 1742 and, except in Peking where the Jesuits had great influence, many priests were martyred or compelled to leave the country. Finally all missionaries were expelled from China—and thus came to an end until the later nineteenth century apostolic work in China.

The persecutions continued until 1820 and thousands of Chinese Catholics, sometimes after horrible torture, gave up their lives for the Faith. Nowhere was there greater Christian heroism than in Korea. In 1842 the Jesuits were allowed to return to the Far East and freedom was granted to missioners to renew their labors. Their stations were again attacked during the Boxer Rebellion of 1900 but their work continued. Until war broke out with Japan in 1937 Catholicism was making remarkable headway among the Chinese. There were two native religious orders of men and the Catholic press issued three publications to the Chinese. In 1926 Rome appointed six Chinese bishops and by 1942 the Chinese government had a minister at the Vatican. Before the advance of Communism in the 1950's China had two thousand native-born priests, and more than three million Catholics—a small percentage of the total population, to be sure, but nonetheless it represented a great missionary triumph over immense odds. The appointment of six vicars apostolic to the Far East ended the Portuguese monopoly, and encouraged the entrance of secular and regular priests to the missions.

In 1638 Pope Urban VIII created the Bishopric of Babylon. French missionaries worked in the Middle East where they converted many natives and slaves. Franciscans and Jesuits worked in Indo-China, Siam, Macao, and the Dutch East Indies. In Manila, the Dominican college of Santo Tomás was established in 1611 and became a Pontifical University later. The Jesuit College of San José, founded in 1601, became the chief center of learning in the Philippines. Franciscans opened the big leper hospital at San Lázaro (1633) and worked to convert in the Celebes. There were Jesuit missionaries in Mindanao, the Moluccas and on Guam, but in the South Pacific some ten thousand Christians died in the great massacres of 1635.

As early as the end of the fifteenth century missionary activity had been going on in Africa, where the Portuguese were the pioneers. Through them the Jesuits, Capuchins and Dominicans were sent to West Coast settlements and to Mozambique between 1596 and 1614. The See of Salvador, established in 1595, served as their base of operations as they traveled into Equatorial Africa. Remarkable results were forthcoming from Jesuit missionary work in Ethiopia or Abyssinia. But when attempts were made to eliminate the national liturgy developed there, the new emperor re-established the Monophysite religion and expelled the Jesuits. This mission did not realize all that was hoped for it, but it gave many martyrs to the Church in the seventeenth century.

By the end of the sixteenth century nearly all religious orders had missionaries in Africa but progress was slow, owing to such obstacles as climate, hostile Moslems, suspicion of foreigners and colonial rivalry among the Dutch, Spanish and Portuguese. Worse still was the hatred of the white man engendered in the natives by the slave traders. By the end of the eighteenth century priests could be found only at the trading centers and in West Africa.

It is in the nineteenth century that a splendid revival of missionary activity began in Africa—an activity that makes it today almost the principal field of missionary work. As the continent was partitioned after the explorations of Stanley and Livingstone, the European powers with colonial interests sent missionaries to look after the well-being of the natives. The needs of Africa gave rise to some of the new purely missionary orders such as the Fathers of the Holy Ghost (1842), the Society for the African Missions (1859), the English Society of St. Joseph (1866) and the White Fathers of Cardinal Lavigerie (1868).

The outstanding figure in African missionary work was Cardinal Lavigerie (1825-92), Archbishop of Algiers, through whose efforts the slave trade was declared unlawful. The two orders he founded, the White Fathers and the White Sisters, did untold good in the work of conversion and care of the natives.

Today this fruitful missionary center, a continent surging with nationalism and new activity, has a Catholic population of five million, more than a hundred bishops, forty-five hundred priests, taken from thirty-four religious orders, three apostolic vicariates, six dioceses, and many thousands of missionary nuns. The primacy of France in African missionary work during the nineteenth and early twentieth century is undenied. In France there was devised and organized the Association for the Propagation of the Faith (1835), which is still today the principal support of all the missions throughout the world. From papal solicitude for the foreign missions came the Congregation, the Collegium Urbanum (an international seminary in Rome), and the Paris Seminary of Foreign Missions.

The nineteenth century, then, which was a century of Catholic losses and trials in the countries of Europe, was at the same time the century in which the Faith was at last carried to every part of the earth.

XXVI

The Era of the French Revolution

In the period between the Treaty of Westphalia (1648) and the outbreak of the French Revolution (1789) the Catholic Church was at war with two tendencies which had become widespread after the Protestant revolt—royal absolutism and nationalism. The first of these has disappeared from Western civilization but the second is still with us. The Church suffered in these struggles with absolutism and nationalism, but in the later tranquil period she emerged far stronger for the trials endured. Contemporary with these assaults, certain new heresies appeared, which added to her troubles.

During the Catholic revival in the centuries between the Council of Trent and the French Revolution the Church regained much ground lost during the early sixteenth century. Under Jesuit leadership, Poland and several German states became Catholic again. A group of reforming Popes beginning with the Dominican monk, Pius V (1566-72), made obedience to the Council of Trent the one rule of their lives. Everywhere colleges were founded and seminaries organized for the training of priests. There was vigorous enforcement of the Council's decrees, especially those on discipline. Through the work of St. Vincent de Paul (1576-1660) the number of hospitals and houses of charity increased greatly. He was the founder of the

Vincentian Fathers (1632), an order which taught and assisted the poor in remote regions of rural France.

There is other evidence that the inner vitality of the Catholic Church showed itself during the period of the eighteenth century. Two years after the Jesuits had been suppressed, when royal absolutism seemed to prevail triumphantly, there died in Rome an Italian priest, Paolo Francesco Danei, known in the Church calendar as St. Paul of the Cross, the founder of the Passionist Fathers, an order of religious renowned like the first St. Paul for the austerity of their lives and the zeal of their preaching of Christ crucified. Another great saint of the period, who was the founder of another great preaching congregation, was St. Alphonsus Ligouri, born near Naples in 1696. His congregation of the Most Holy Redeemer or the Redemptorist Fathers was especially committed to the spiritual care of the most neglected in the Italian population, the rural poor. St. Alphonsus himself preferred to work among the goatherds in the mountainous regions. He was perhaps the greatest authority on moral theology and the author of many books of Marian devotions, such as *The Glories of Mary*. When he died in 1787, on the eve of the French Revolution, he could boast that after a long life of hearing confessions he had never dismissed a penitent unabsolved.

The fragments of the Jesuit order surviving in Prussia and White Russia managed to preserve the form and spirit of the Ignatian rule during this trying period while they hopefully awaited the order's restoration. Meanwhile there were experiments in setting up associations similar in spirit and aims to the Society of Jesus. One of the first of these began in Belgium as the Society of the Sacred Heart of Jesus; when the French Revolution drove the Society underground it moved to Austria. Though it had a brief history, it holds an important place in modern church history. One of its members was Father Joseph Varin, who became a Jesuit when the Society of Jesus was restored by Rome. His scholarship and skill as a spiritual director, a rather severe one at that, might not of themselves have preserved his memory. As in the case of other devoted teachers who have been outshone by brilliant pupils, we recall Father Varin because he formed and trained a modern saint whose name holds a prominent place in the history of education. This was St. Madeleine Sophie Barat, foundress of the Religious of the Sacred Heart.[67]

During the pre-Revolutionary period, however, though France produced such impressive achievements in that highest of all forms of human activity, holiness, she was also the scene of the severest trials the Church had to face. Lutheranism gained no foothold there but Calvinism was adhered to tenaciously by the French Huguenots. For thirty years of the sixteenth century the French Catholics and Huguenots were engaged in wars of religion which became, like the Thirty Years' War, brutal contests for political power as well. In 1572 the queen-regent, Catherine de Medici, a Catholic fanatic, ordered the massacre of Protestants on St. Bartholomew's Eve, which she justified on the basis of an imaginary plot against her son's throne. This serves as the only explanation for the deplorable rejoicing in Rome when the news of the massacres reached that city.

The French crown passed eventually to the Protestant king, Henry IV of Navarre. In 1593 he was reconverted to Catholicism in what may have been an act of political expediency. Nevertheless it brought the senseless fighting to an end. Thereafter France followed a policy of reli-

gious toleration. Henry IV proclaimed the Edict of
Nantes in 1598, which gave religious liberty and sanc-
tuary to the Huguenots in some two hundred fortified
towns until the edict was revoked by Louis XIV in
1685. Protestantism would not again disturb seriously
the Catholic Church in France. Her troubles would
arise from among her own children.

Calvin's doctrine of human depravity and God's
predestination had been condemned by the Church for
a long time but his teaching reappeared among French
Catholics in a modified form in the heresy propounded
by the Dutch theologian, Cornelius Jansen (1585-
1638), the bishop of Ypres in Flanders. Jansen was
an earnest cleric, unaware of the unsoundness of the
doctrines he held. Within the Catholic system Jansenism
was a heresy almost as injurious to the old spirit and
constitution as the doctrines of Luther himself. Jansen
denied the freedom of the will, the possibility of resisting grace and the belief that Christ had died for all men,
and he maintained that it was impossible for man to
keep some of God's commandments for man cannot
by free will avoid sin. This heresy gained a wide following in France, where it is sometimes called Catholic
Calvinism. Many heretics demonstrated a great piety
and austerity, yet their Jansenism formed a body of
gloomy beliefs and practices whose harshness pervaded
theological teaching for a century.

Jansenist influence lingered in France longer than
anywhere else, and perhaps it has not yet wholly disappeared. The powerful French minister and virtual
ruler of France, Cardinal Richelieu (1585-1642), who
was the heresy's enemy, imprisoned many of Jansen's
followers. The *Augustinus,* Jansen's book published
posthumously in 1640, which contained most of his
views, was condemned by Rome along with other

Jansenist works. The Jesuits fought these teachings with books, pamphlets, sermons and spiritual direction, which drew from them the enmity of Jansenism's most gifted convert, Blaise Pascal, mathematical genius, religious philosopher, master of French prose and author of the *Provincial Letters* against the Jesuits. These were brilliant, witty, amusing and, as propaganda, unscrupulous. They did the French Jesuits much harm.[68] When Clement XI (1700-21) issued his final condemnation of Jansenism in 1713, the Catholics of France divided into two great parties, the Jansenists and their opponents. The division also came to distinguish those who supported the Pope and those who opposed him.

Even in those countries like France which remained Catholic there was a feeling of national opposition to Rome. This was demonstrated in efforts by lay rulers to prevent any interference by the Pope in their temporal affairs. In France the clergy had been developing a tradition of independence for centuries and they even tried to limit the influence of the Pope in spiritual affairs. During the reign of the "Sun King," Louis XIV (1643-1715), king and clergy united against the Pope, thereby threatening to produce a schism. This attitude of king and clergy is called Gallicanism. In defying papal authority Gallicanism had kinship with Jansenism. Often, however, Gallicanism was more a state of mind than a definite doctrine; its origins can be traced back to the Middle Ages but it made a fresh appearance after Jansenist teachings were condemned by three successive Popes in the seventeenth century. Jansenism as a body of doctrine faded into the background of French religious thought but Gallicanism, which had come to life during the controversy, caused trouble when Louis XIV was king.

Louis quarreled with Rome because he insisted on his right to collect all revenues and to exercise the appointive power when episcopal sees fell vacant. Pope Clement X denied he had such rights. Thereupon the king summoned an assembly of the clergy to support him and defy the Pope. This body was under the leadership of Jacques-Bénigne Bossuet (1627-1704), the Bishop of Meaux, an eloquent pulpit orator who also served as the tutor to the future Louis XV. He desired to effect the reunion of Christendom by making every lawful concession to the Protestants, thus depriving them of their strongest arguments against the Catholic Church. He composed the Four Gallican Articles of 1682 and continued to defend them even after they had been abandoned by the King. Bossuet was the author of the famous *Catechism,* in which he enunciated the theory of royal absolutism and divine right monarchy which Louis XIV used as the basis of his rule.

The Four Gallican Articles, drawn up by Bossuet and the French clergy, were designed to settle the basic question of papal authority. Recognizing the primacy of the Bishops of Rome, Bossuet, however, denied that the Pope had any authority over civil affairs. He denied the power of the Pope to depose rulers and declared the supremacy of ecumenical councils over the Pope.

Louis XIV ordered the French clergy to accept and teach these articles in the seminaries throughout France. Pope Innocent XI then annulled the proceedings of the Assembly. Three successive Popes condemned the Articles and refused to approve any episcopal appointments in France. In 1693 Louis XIV was finally forced to yield to Rome. He withdrew his edict compelling acceptance of the Four Articles. The Pope then confirmed the King's nominees and peace was restored.

The papal victory in this matter was more apparent than real. The seminaries continued to teach the Gallican articles, which were generally accepted by the French clergy and laity. Only the Jesuits took a strong stand against them—one of the reasons for their Society's suppression in the eighteenth century. Moreover, Gallicanism was adopted by other Catholic rulers in Europe. Doctrine and practice differed from country to country, but Gallicanism was widely professed in France and Flanders during the eighteenth century and spread to Ireland and England. It is still professed by the heretical sect called Old Catholics. In Spain it was manifested by the increased use of the Inquisition for political rather than religious purposes. In all countries the divine origin of princely power was taught, and the Pope was held to be the elected head of the Church, limited like a constitutional monarch.[69]

Despite his quarrel with Rome, Louis XIV never wavered in his opposition to the Jansenists. After his reconciliation with the Papacy he sought its co-operation along with that of the French bishops and the Jesuits against the heretics. Now the Jansenists became the defenders of extreme Gallicanism and found some support among the lower clergy. Though the monarchy repudiated Gallicanism, the justices of the royal courts continued to oppose Rome and allied themselves with the Jansenists. This situation divided Catholic France in the eighteenth century, making it less difficult for the anticlerical rationalists, who were the opponents of all revealed religion, to make headway.

During the quarter of a century before the Revolution, the Church was subjected to a new attack in Germany. Bishop Johann Nicholas von Hontheim of Treves, writing under the pen name Febronius (1701-90), tried to revive the old imperial claims to dominate the Papacy.

He favored the formation of a national church and maintained that the Holy See was not superior to the rest of the bishops as a body or to a general council. When his book was condemned by Rome he made a retraction and died peacefully some years later. But his doctrine achieved popularity at the courts of certain Catholic sovereigns, notably Joseph II of Austria (1741-90), who tried to carry out a program based on the ideas of Febronius. He forbade communications between the Austrian bishops and Rome. All Church decrees, including papal pronouncements, required his approval. This reforming son of the great Empress, Maria Theresa, seemed to regard the Church as a department of his civil service, and he carried his interference in its affairs to a ridiculous degree by prescribing the number of candles to be placed on the altars, regulating the length of sermons and ordering specified hymns. For all this foolishness, Frederick the Great of Prussia contemptuously referred to Joseph II as "my cousin, the sacristan."

The Revolution which inflamed France in 1789 affected the Catholic Church in all parts of Europe. In this great outburst of pent-up hatred against the old order, absolute monarchy, its abuses and the nobility, the Church unfortunately suffered. Before the first year of the Revolution ended, the Church in France had lost all its main sources of income. Tithes were abolished and Church property was seized by the state. Those moderate reformers in the first stage of the Revolution were determined to reorganize the Church along national lines and force its conformity to state policy.

On August 4, 1789, by vote of the National Assembly the Church of France lost all its privileges and exemptions. On October 10, 1789, Talleyrand, who was at that time still Bishop of Autun, made the proposal that the nation take over the Church's property, capital and revenues. In 1790 the Assembly abolished all the monastic orders; commissioners were sent out in February to "liberate the monks and nuns." By the end of that year all the religious communities had disappeared. The sale of all Church property was ordered and inventories were drawn up. The secular clergymen were to continue their services to the faithful. However, the Assembly adopted the fatal measure known as the Civil Constitution of the Clergy, the work of the Gallican and Jansenist lawyers. Under it, the dioceses of France were to be rearranged and the bishops were to be elected by the people. The secular clergy were men paid salaries by the state provided they agreed to sever their connections with the Pope. All future bishops and priests were henceforth to be elected by representatives of the laity.

When, in October, 1790, ninety-three bishops denounced the law, the Assembly ordered all clerics to swear an oath to the new constitution being drawn up for the nation. Left with no guidance, the clergymen at first almost evenly divided on the matter. Those who refused the oath were dispossessed. Then, in April of 1791, the Pope of Rome finally ruled on the situation with a condemnation of the Civil Constitution of the Clergy and a prohibition to take the oath. Now, all over France the persecution of the nonjurant clergy and their adherents was begun. Catholics everywhere in France, and especially in the Vendée, refused the ministrations of the government priests. Clergymen faithful to Rome were hunted down, imprisoned, exiled or sent to the guillotine. 1792 saw the massacres of priest-prisoners all over France and, more mercifully, wholesale deportations.

The government supported the constitutional Church composed of the bishops and priests who accepted the law of 1790. However, the Church was stripped of all its sacred vessels, statues, pictures and vestments, its liturgy was changed and the celibacy of the clergy was abolished. Finally, the cult of reason was inaugurated to replace Catholicism, and an actress was enthroned as the Goddess of Reason on the high altar of the Cathedral of Notre Dame in 1793.

During all this, the true Church, though suffering persecution, benefited from the strengthening of religious devotion. The Directory which governed after 1795 was milder and after 1797 some twelve thousand priests were allowed to return to France. But within a few months vandalism broke out once again. The great abbey church of Cluny, second only to St. Peter's in Rome, was razed to the ground, as were the cathedrals of Liège, Cambrai and Bruges. Napoleon's troops arrived just in time to prevent the cathedral of Antwerp from suffering a similar fate.

The *coup d'état* of 1799 brought Napoleon Bonaparte to power. Almost immediately following his great victory at Marengo, he informed the newly elected Pope Pius VII (1800-23) that he stood ready to reinstate Catholicism in France. The outcome of a meeting between the Pontiff and ruler was the Concordat of 1801. The Pope, of course, wished to restore Catholic life to its full vigor in France through the Mass, sacraments and the recruitment of new priests to fill the ranks left empty by death, exile and apostasy. Napoleon wanted to restore unity to France and use the Church as an instrument of his absolute government. Under the Concordat, the state was to appoint the bishops but these appointments had to be approved by the Pope.

Some of the changes made earlier by the Civil Constitution of the Clergy were retained, such as the payment of salaries for the secular clergy; but the Church in France was reunited to the Papacy. The free exercise of the Catholic religion was guaranteed, seminaries were restored, and the cathedrals and churches were returned to the bishops. As a matter of fact, papal control over the French clergy was greater now than it had been before 1789.

On Easter Sunday, in 1802, the Concordat was published and the three consuls who ruled France assisted at a solemn mass of thanksgiving at Notre Dame. The Concordat regulated the fortunes of Catholics in France down to 1905, and served as a model for the general relations between Rome and other European states throughout the nineteenth century.

By the end of 1802, however, Napoleon showed that his real intentions were to regulate the Church in France since he had found it impossible to destroy it. The refusal of Pope Pius VII to make any further concessions and his unwillingness to join Napoleon against Great Britain led to increased friction. The aging Pontiff was forced to go to Paris for the coronation of Napoleon as Emperor of the French. Napoleon and Josephine kept Pius VII waiting for over an hour on the high altar of Notre Dame Cathedral, where eventually Napoleon impatiently seized the imperial crown from the waiting Pope's hands and placed it on his own head! For ten years after 1802 Napoleon marched from victory to victory, unseating ancient kings and ensconcing his relatives on the many thrones left vacant. By 1809 armies occupied the Papal States, which were annexed to the Empire. Pope Pius VII excommunicated the Emperor and for this he was dispossessed of his territories, and taken to France as a prisoner for six years until Napoleon's abdication in 1814.

When the French Revolutionary armies entered Germany in 1792 the prince-bishops fled before the victors and with them disappeared their political importance for all time. One menace to Catholic unity was thus removed. The papal delegate, Cardinal Consalvi, was unable to secure the restoration of the ecclesiastical states in Germany at the Congress of Vienna in 1815, but he won respect for the Papacy and its own Italian territories.

Napoleon had reduced the number of independent states in Germany from 303 to 38. He then organized the Confederation of the Rhine and encouraged the secular rulers to regulate the Church in their states as he was striving to do in France. They continued this policy after Napoleon's downfall in 1814. As a result of the transfers of population, thousands of Catholics now found themselves under Protestant rulers. There were only five bishops in Germany at this time. The first impulse in high ecclesiastical circles was to plan a national independent church. Thanks in large part to the Redemptorist St. Clement Hofbauer, this peril was averted. A series of other concordats was now negotiated between the Holy See and the princes of Bavaria, Prussia, Hanover and the Rhine principalities. Among Protestant as well as Catholic princes the Holy See was recognized as the effective primate of the whole Church.[70]

The French Revolution, with its antireligious campaigns, and the long wars of the Napoleonic period weakened the Church. However, the Revolution swept away the despotism of the *ancien régime*. Many abuses in the Church were ended. The attacks of revolutionaries on the old social order and on the Church won for both new friends even among non-Catholics. Persecution brought the most noble and heroic qualities to the fore. Napoleon's violence to the Pope rehabilitated the Church in the eyes of former enemies like England, where the respect shown the Holy See in its sufferings was remarkable, and where the welcome accorded refugee French clergy was even more remarkable.

The era of the French Revolution and of Napoleon threw Europe into the melting pot. Many had lost their enthusiasm for the irreligious rationalism of the past century which had brought so much suffering and misery. In Germany there began an amazing revival of Catholic life which produced a new generation of humanists and scholars. In France, which continued to serve as the key province of Catholicism, the Viscount de Chateaubriand and other writers described the beauties of the Church and her great contributions to civilization. They preached reverence for the traditions of the past and engendered a new interest in the culture of the Middle Ages. By contrast with the eighteenth-century appeal to reason, these revivalists appealed to man's deepest emotions and sentiments.

Thus the nineteenth century saw the disappearance of many of the old tendencies, a truly remarkable religious revival and the amazing recovery of the Papacy.

XXVII

Revival in the British Isles

By the nineteenth century the Church had become active once more in England and agitated for the full repeal of the penal laws against Catholics. After the Emancipation Act of 1829 Catholics were eligible for all but a very few public offices in the English government and all voting restrictions were removed. The Church was thus left in peace and slowly made headway.

The English hierarchy was restored in 1850. The brilliant leadership of that hierarchy has since enabled the Church not only to increase her numbers (now nearly four million English people profess Catholicism) but to wield an influence greater than those numbers warranted. Though the body of English Catholics remained small throughout the nineteenth century, its unity and discipline were remarkable features.

Thus, in spite of the establishment of the Anglican Church in England and Ireland in the sixteenth century, Catholicism survived in each country. But this triumph was not won without a struggle. Despite religious persecution, expropriation of their lands, bearing excessive taxation for the support of the Established Church, and fines for not attending its services, the Irish Catholics remained faithful to Rome. Nominally they were granted religious freedom in 1691 but Irish Protestants still controlled the Irish Parliament. Catholics were not allowed to vote, enter the professions or even hold land. However, in 1771, when the repeal of these penal laws began, there were well over two million Catholics in Ireland. The founding of English colleges on the continent, like the one at Douai (1568), which trained writers, controversialists and sent priests into England and Ireland, played an important role in this Catholic survival. That the Irish preserved their Catholicism despite the worst oppression was later to be of the greatest importance for the rebirth of the Church in England and still more for its growth in the United States.

Catholics in Ireland gained the right to hold some offices in 1793; a small percentage had the right to vote. Daniel O'Connell was most instrumental in gaining seats for Irish Catholics in the Union Parliament. He, himself, was elected to the House of Commons in 1828 and the London government, fearing the results of refusing him his seat, carried through the Catholic Emancipation Act of 1829. Thereafter Catholics throughout the United Kingdom secured the right to sit in Parliament and hold most high offices.

In 1833 there began in England what is now called the Oxford Movement or what was then called the Tractarian Movement. Leadership of the Tractarians had passed to a young Anglican clergyman, John Henry Newman. While traveling in Italy that year, he had met Monsignor Nicholas Wiseman, rector of the English College at Rome. The deep spiritual awakening of the Oxford Movement was turned to the advantage of the Catholic Church by Monsignor Wiseman. In 1835, and again in 1839, he visited England and preached to mixed congregations of Catholics and Protestants. There were nearly half a million Catholics in England in 1840—a fact partly due to his influence.

Newman was charmed by the sincerity, scholarship and enthusiasm of this scholarly churchman. After returning to England, Newman and a number of his associates at Oxford University started their movement to raise the spiritual level of the Church of England.

Some of the leaders of this movement devoted their entire lives to this original purpose. Many others, including Frederick Oakeley, William Ward and Newman, came to believe that the Roman Catholic was the one true Church. A dozen years after the Oxford Movement had begun, Newman, to use Disraeli's colorful phrase, struck the blow under which the Establishment still reels. On a stormy night in October, 1845, he submitted to Rome at the feet of Father Dominic, an Italian Passionist missionary, thus setting an example for many intellectuals of his and later generations. These intellectuals, and most of all Newman himself, who was made a cardinal in 1879, gave to the Church in England a great wing of learned men. In Newman, the Catholic Church acquired her greatest modern defender and apologist in the English tongue.[71]

In 1850, Pope Pius IX (1846-78) decided the time was ripe to re-establish the hierarchy in England, for since the Protestant revolt the country had been a mission era under the Congregation of Propaganda, with her Catholic population ruled by eight vicars-apostolic. The cardinal's hat was given to Dr. Nicholas Patrick Wiseman, who thus assumed headship of the new hierarchy as Cardinal Archbishop of Westminster. This plump, erudite, good-natured churchman was shocked by the fierce antipapal riots in which windows were smashed, bonfires were lighted in the streets, and both the Pope and new cardinal-archbishop were burned in effigy. However, Wiseman was equal to the task. In his sincere and temperate tone, he penned an *Appeal to the English People* which soothed hot tempers. The storm subsided as quickly as it had arisen. Wiseman was friend to new converts as well as "old" Catholics, and his diplomacy united both groups in the common effort to allay Protestant suspicion. When he died in 1865, Londoners lined the streets by the tens of thousands to witness his funeral procession.

The most famous convert after Newman was the Anglican Archdeacon of Chichester, Henry Manning, who was converted in 1851. Pope Pius IX appointed him dean of the Cathedral Chapter of Westminster (1857) and he succeeded Cardinal Wiseman as head of the English hierarchy in 1865. Ten years later he was elevated to the cardinalate.

In the years before the middle of the nineteenth century a wave of hopefulness spread over the Church, premature as events proved. In Germany, Catholicism was enjoying a renaissance with the great prelate, Bishop Ketteler, as its inspiration. In England the Catholic converts were dreaming of a "second spring" to precede a corporate return of Anglicans to Roman unity. French Gallicanism was discredited by the remarkable Abbé Felicité Robert de Lamennais, who saw in the alliance of Church and state the source of all the wrongs in the world of the Church at that time. After he had done his best work he left the Church, but his former friends and allies, Montalembert and Lacordaire, the restorer of the Dominican Order in France, seemed to be forming a happy alliance between the orthodox Catholic Faith and the new political democracy, together with an awakened social conscience.[72]

During these troubled years, the spiritual life of the Church was touched by the experience of the young peasant girl, St. Bernadette Soubirous, who saw her visions of the Blessed Virgin in the cave at Lourdes in 1858. Some months later, there died in France a country priest, badly educated, whimsical, practicing a terrifying asceticism in his personal life, an alleged miracle worker and a genius in directing consciences. He was Jean-Baptiste Vianney; we know him as a canonized saint, the Curé d'Ars.

In 1896 the Anglicans closest in their views to Rome sought from the Holy Father recognition of the validity of the Anglican Holy Orders. The Pope denied the Anglican claims. Thereafter some Anglicans came over to Rome; others became irreconcilable and still others renewed their efforts to secure a reunion with the Holy See.

All the remaining limitations on English Catholics were removed in the twentieth century except succession to the throne. The strong, well-organized body of over four million English Catholics, to whom Cardinal Newman and Father Frederick William Faber introduced St. Philip Neri's Congregation of the Oratory, have increased their activity in every sphere of religious endeavor. Despite her relatively small Catholic population, England has made her contribution to the missionary effort through the English Society of St. Joseph at Mill Hill, north of London, which has undertaken work along lines similar to the Paris Institut des Missions Étrangères.

XXVIII

The Church in the Nineteenth Century

By tying itself to reaction under Napoleon in France, under Metternich in Austria and again under Louis Napoleon, the Catholic Church had placed itself in an unfavorable light with the revolutionaries in Europe who rose up to defy conservatism, especially in 1830 and 1848. To them the Church was the fattest target in sight. Widespread disaffection with religious claims accompanied these revolts.[73] Catholicism had virtually abdicated its direction of social life, now controlling only the weak, on whom it imposed obedience, while it extolled the rights of rulers.

To free the Church from its association with unpopular and reactionary governments was one of the aims of Catholic liberals. After the fall of Napoleon, who had reduced the Pope to subserviency with his haughty statement, "I am your Emperor," there were many within the Church who came to argue for the separation of Church and state, after making concessions to the new liberal currents.[74] The leaders who spearheaded this tactical liberalism were the Frenchmen, Count de Montalembert, Father Lamennais and Father Lacordaire. They knew that society was becoming more democratic and that the Church could best carry on its mission by identifying itself with the new currents of reform. They believed that the separation of Church and state would make possible a greater Catholic impact on the fortunes of France.

The Papacy, attracted by the Ultramontane strategy, at first seemed ready to extend its hand to their effort. Soon the Pope was embarrassed and was shaking his fist at them. Their premature attempt to reconcile Catholicism and revolutionary principles aroused bitter antagonism. Gregory XVI (1831-46) condemned their paper *L'Avenir* (The Future) in 1832. In a now famous encyclical entitled *Mirari Vos* (1832), the theories of these liberal Catholics were also condemned, although neither Lamennais nor his collaborators were mentioned. For Lamennais the shock of disavowal by Rome was too much; he left the Church. Montalembert and Father Lacordaire conformed to the Church's teaching and continued their work, playing important roles in the revival of Catholicism in France under the July monarchy (1830-48).

During the reign of Pope Pius IX (1846-78), the longest in the history of the Papacy, the Church once again came to be tied to reaction. The events of 1848, the *Communist Manifesto,* the Socialist front, the workers' uprising, the three French revolutions in forty years, and the political division in that nation which had the effect of dividing the Catholic forces in their struggles for religious liberty—all these set the tone for the next century. Pius IX's defensive position against liberalism was hardened into his *Syllabus of Errors* (1864) which attacked the "error" that "the Church ought to be separated from the state and the state from the Church."

Pius IX erected a total of 29 archbishoprics and 132 bishoprics. As the steamship and railroad made worldwide communication easier, a closer union developed between the individual churches and the ecclesiastical center, Rome. Now the faithful thronged to the Holy City in numbers never seen before. In 1854, when the great impetus was given to Marian devotions in the Church by the formal declaration of the doctrine of the Immaculate Conception of the Blessed Virgin Mary as an article of faith, and in 1862, at the canonization of the first martyrs of the Japanese Church, Pius IX saw himself surrounded by a gathering of the princes of the Church which surpassed all former ecumenical councils. In 1867, when the Pope celebrated the eighteenth centenary of the deaths of the Apostles, Peter and Paul, about five hundred bishops were in attendance.[75]

By the time Pius IX died (1878), the divided Catholics of France found themselves face to face with the development of the Third Republic into the classic example of a persecuting liberal state, bereft of real leadership, lay or ecclesiastical—a misfortune that was to deprive the masterly guidance of Leo XIII of half its value.[76]

The movement for Italian unification had its beginnings during the Napoleonic period, when the western portion of the Papal States was annexed to France, and the eastern portion was formed into the kingdom of Italy. In 1815 the Congress of Vienna recognized the historic rights of the Italian princes and the Papal States were restored to the Holy See.

A number of moderates and revolutionaries in Italy opposed the restoration; they sought not only liberal reforms but also national unification. When the reforming efforts of Pope Gregory XVI failed to bring peace, Austria and then France intervened to preserve order. Their occupation lasted until 1838.

A number of new reforms were introduced but they did not satisfy the groups demanding Italian unification. Mazzini, the founder of the society "Young Italy," favored a republic with its capital at Rome. Some favored a unified monarchy under the king of Sardinia; still others favored the program of Vincenzo Gioberti, a Sardinian priest who proposed a federation of Italian principalities under the leadership of the Pope.

The course of events took an unexpected turn outside the Papal States. Radicals in Italy took over the movement for unification and set up republics in Rome and other states. Louis Napoleon restored Pius IX to power in Rome in the summer of 1849, after which the Pope withdrew most of his concessions. Garibaldi, a successor of Mazzini in the short-lived Roman Republic of 1860, later conquered Naples, which then voted for union with Sardinia, Tuscany, Modena and Parma. In spite of the presence of French troops in Rome, Napoleon III agreed to Sardinia's taking over the entire eastern portion of the Papal States. In 1861 the new kingdom of Italy was proclaimed. When Prussia went to war with France in 1870, Napoleon had to withdraw his troops from Rome and the remaining territory of the Papal States was incorporated into Italy.

On the same day that he issued his *Syllabus of Errors,* Pius IX suggested to his advisers the calling of a general council—the first since Trent. The next five years were given over to preparation for the meeting, which opened at the Vatican on December 8, 1869. Its major aim was to restate the doctrines of the Church to a world becoming increasingly hostile to Rome, both politically and intellectually.

One of the questions in dispute was the doctrine of Papal infallibility. It was brought into the Council, where it was thoroughly examined. Out of this came the doctrine that the Roman Pontiff cannot err when defining ex cathedra a doctrine concerning faith and morals. Such doctrines as the Pope proclaims are to be held by the whole Church. When, in October, 1870, Italian troops were storming Rome, Pope Pius adjourned the Council meetings. Since that day it has neither been reassembled nor dissolved, but its decrees were accepted by the majority of Catholics throughout the world.

In 1871, Italy passed a law of Papal Guarantees, assuring the Pope a fixed income, freedom to communicate with the outside world and spiritual independence. Pius IX rejected the offer on the basis that papal territorial rights had been set aside and territory seized without his consent. Now the Pope became a voluntary prisoner of the Vatican and forbade Catholics to take any role in Italian political life. This arrangement lasted until the signing of the Concordat and the Lateran treaty of 1929 with Mussolini's government, which created an independent Vatican City and recognized the Pope as its sovereign.

In the new German Empire created by Otto von Bismarck in 1871, there was official and popular opposition to the dogma of papal infallibility. The real leader of the anti-infallibility party was a learned Bavarian Catholic priest, Dr. Johann von Döllinger. After his renunciation of the dogma, many of his followers seceded from the Church to found a sect known as "the Old Catholics."

Bismarck saw Catholic investment in Germany as an intrusion on German national claims. When the Old Catholics were not permitted to teach in the universities and were excommunicated, Bismarck came to their defense. In 1872 he launched his *"kulturkampf,"* or "battle of the civilization," which was really a struggle between the German chancellor and Pope.

The agitation reached its peak with the anti-Catholic education laws (Falk laws) of 1873. They were condemned by Rome but the National Liberal Party and all anticlericals in Germany embraced these measures as part of the great cultural struggle by a new, vibrant national state against the Church.

However, Bismarck became too aggressive and Catholic opposition rallied behind Ludwig Windthorst, the leader of the Catholic Center Party, which became so powerful by 1877 that Bismarck had to seek its help in carrying through liberal legislation to undercut the Socialist agitation which was a growing menace to his power. Bismarck made overtures to the new Pope, Leo XIII, in 1878 and the repeal of anti-Catholic laws began in 1879. Much ground that had been lost was regained for Catholicism and the prestige of the Pope was enhanced when peace came to Germany through Rome.

As Father Hughes has written of the years to 1870:

> The period ends . . . with the papacy finally routed as a temporal power, destroyed . . . by the Liberal States. The downfall of the papal States in 1870 is a kind of symbol that the process begun at Westphalia in 1648 has reached its climax. At the same time, the Vatican Council of that same year testifies to the final triumph within the Church itself of the old Roman conception of the papal office. Henceforth there will be no Gallicanism, even in name, even as a school of ecclesiastical politics. And . . . there will be a new type of pope. . . . The popes of the nineteenth century . . . (1800- 1878) are all of them good men, and several are men of real ability. But they are all men

of the eighteenth century, or rather of the ab-
solutist age of which that century is . . . the
symbol. None of them really understood the
new world which the Revolution had produced,
understood either how to fight it or how to convert it.[77]

But upon the death of Pius IX there was elected
a Pope "supremely gifted in political understanding
as in the diplomatic gifts." This man was Leo XIII
(1878-1903), regarded by some as the greatest papal
ruler since Paul III, a traditionalist and a conservative
who thought in modern terms and spoke in the modern
idiom, and whose long reign is the beginning of a new
age of Catholic history.[78]

The new Pope came to office with his main objectives
already set and with definite plans for their attainment.
In the political affairs of Italy there was no change;
the Pope remained the "prisoner" of the Vatican, but
he began to display a world-wide activity. "The cheerful
bonhomie of Pius IX gave place to the steely determination of a pope who seemed pure intelligence, all
mind, who could work at his desk ten and twelve hours
a day, week in, week out, for years on end."[79] One of
the first prelates of the nineteenth century to be fully
convinced that liberalism had come to stay, he was
determined to show Catholics how to live in a liberal
world, and still maintain their Catholic principles.

In this era of intellectual and social ferment, the
spirit of Leo's action in the Church was breathed into
his great encyclicals. They may be studied with profit
for, unlike most Popes, Leo XIII proceeded to use
the Holy See as a professional chair from which to
address Catholics throughout the world, and ultimately
many who were not Catholic. For a quarter of a century

he issued encyclical after encyclical on the great intellectual and social questions of the day.

Quod Apostolici Muneris (1878) deals with the subject of socialism. In *Aeterni Patris* (1879) Pope Leo XIII showed his determination to base Catholic philosophy, especially that which was part of the education of clergymen, on the teachings of Aristotle as they were assimilated and synthesized by St. Thomas Aquinas. He encouraged the revival of Scholasticism as the first step in the reconquest of the world for Christ. *Diuturnum Illud* (1881) and *Immortale Dei* (1885) dealt with the role of the state, the subject of legitimate authority in the state, and the sources of legitimate authority.

Finally, in 1891 came the greatest of all these papal documents, the classic *Rerum Novarum*. Sometimes referred to as "The Workingman's Encyclical," it is a treatise on the whole social problem in all its aspects —the obligations and acceptable mutual relations of capital and labor, the rights of workers to voluntary association and collective bargaining, and their ethical claim to a living wage and reasonable leisure. According to Leo XIII, justice also requires that the employers be guaranteed a fair income from their property; however, he emphasized that in attaining this fair income, labor should be treated with human dignity, and that special consideration be given women and children employees.[80]

Monopoly, the abuses of capitalism and industrial slavery came under the papal condemnation as wholly as Marxian Communism. Leo XIII did indeed speak with disapproval of "socialism," but he referred to the Marxism of the two Internationales, not to the Christian Democratic socialism of modern Italy or France or the moderate element in the British Labour Party. He went still further by saying that mutual arrangements made by capital and labor are preferable but the state has the right to protect workingmen and to intervene in labor problems in order to secure justice for all. He warned, however, that the state cannot absorb individuals, that the workingman has the right to form unions, and that these associations should perform their proper functions for the workingmen rather than have the state take them over.

Here was a forthright, courageous analysis of difficult social problems announced far in advance of their time by a Pope who enjoyed a world-wide prestige never before attained. It is no exaggeration to say that all modern labor leaders such as the energetic Catholic layman, Terence Powderly, who organized the Knights of Labor, believed in and worked for was summed up in *Rerum Novarum*—in the excellent Latin of Pope Leo XIII, who wrote all his own encyclicals.[81]

When Pope Leo XIII died, in the early years of the new century (July 20, 1903), he left behind him a Church whose life and multifarious activities had been renewed like the Psalmist's youth—*ut aquila*, "as an eagle." Critical years lay ahead and Catholics would perceive a guiding Providence in a pontificate that built up reserves of spiritual strength and of initiative in all kinds of religious enterprises: the encyclicals on the Holy Ghost (*Divinum Illud*), the Holy Eucharist (*Mirae Caritatis*); the fifteen encyclicals on the devotion to the Holy Rosary; the consecration to the Sacred Heart of Jesus of the whole human race; the institution and development of the Eucharistic Congresses; the extension of the Foreign Missions; the encyclical on Biblical studies and the establishment of the Biblical Commission; the letter on the duty of Catholics to be wholly truthful historians; the throwing open to the scholars of the world of the secret archives of the Vatican; the foundation of new Catholic universities at Fribourg and Washington, D.C., and of the Institute of Thomist philosophy at Louvain, and the immense expansion of the hierarchy. Never, since the time of Pope Paul III (1534-49) had the Sacred College included such an array of great personalities, among them Cardinal Newman.[82]

XXIX

The Church in Latin America

The first expedition of Columbus to the New World landed on an island in the Bahamas which the discoverer christened San Salvador in honor of the Savior of mankind. Columbus, as we know, died with the conviction that he had reached the Far East. In the years which followed his four expeditions, all expeditions to the new lands were accompanied by priests as chaplains—Franciscans, Dominicans, Augustinians, in the early years, Jesuits in the later half of the century. Secular clergy, too, began to build up a new Catholicism from California to the Argentine. Sees were established almost as soon as the news of the Spanish conquests reached Rome. Cities grew, churches and cathedrals were built, hospitals and convents were founded, and the first universities—in 1538 the University of Santo Tomas de Aquino at Santo Domingo; in 1553 the University of Mexico City; and in 1578 San Marcos in Lima.

The struggle to win the natives of the New World into Christ's Church went on and prospered despite the cruelty of the conquerors. From the very beginning, missionaries fought for the welfare of their helpless native flocks. In this they were encouraged by the Popes; in 1537 Pope Paul III, in a famous bull, declared that the Indians were as much human beings as their new masters and enjoyed the same natural rights, which

237

their lords would have to respect. Ramifying the efforts of missionaries abroad was the work of professors at the Catholic universities in Spain. The Dominican, Francis of Victoria (1480-1546), set forth in some detail the natural rights of the Indians and the limits of royal power in their regard.

The struggle to establish Catholicism in the New World met with great success, and with it came the first American saints: St. Toribio de Mogrovejo (1538-1616); the Franciscan missionary, St. Francis of Solano (1549-1610), whose preaching converted the Indians of the Chaco by the thousands; the Dominican nun, St. Rose of Lima (1586-1617), born on American soil, as was the Dominican lay brother, Blessed Martin de Porres, son of a Spanish father and a Negro mother, born in Lima, Peru, where he spent his life serving the sick and suffering natives; the Jesuit St. Peter Claver (1581-1654), patron of Catholic missions among Negroes, who devoted his life to redeeming Negro slaves for Christ in Colombia; St. Louis Bertrand (1526-82), a Spanish Dominican who worked among the natives of Colombia and Panama, and many others. The saints who have labored in South America are greatly honored by the Catholics of that continent, where many religious orders still devote themselves to planting the seeds of sanctity.

The effort to shield the American natives from their oppressive masters led the Jesuits to take an active role in South American missionary work. In 1549 St. Ignatius Loyola sent Father Manoel de Nobrega to Brazil, where he protested against the enslavement of natives on the sugar plantations near Bahia. Father José de Anchieta, another Jesuit, was also sent to southern Brazil, where he established the College of São Paulo in 1554. This marked the beginnings of

Brazil's great southern city. From this base the Jesuits pushed into Paraguay, where they established their famous "reductions" for the Guarani Indians, which made their district a virtual Arcady. These reductions were settlements of communities consisting of hundreds of Indians and they were designed and managed by the Jesuit Fathers, who excluded from them all non-Indians. The first settlement was founded in 1609. The aim of the reductions (from the Latin *"reduco"*) was to provide the means whereby the Indians could be "led back" from heathenism.

The center of the reduction was the church, with its missionaries, nuns, school and hospital. The manual labor was distributed among the natives and supervised, and the whole community was cared for under a paternalistic system, which has evoked comparison with the City of God on earth. By 1750 there were nearly 100,000 Indians living in these reductions. In the course of the suppression of the Society of Jesus, there is no more painful chapter than the order of Charles III expelling all the Jesuits from America in 1767 and abolishing the reductions. The constant rivalry between civil authorities and religious leaders prompted the order. In his concept of regalistic control, Charles III resented what he regarded as an empire within an empire. As events proved, his apprehension was exaggerated. His act may have pleased some of the rivals and enemies of the Jesuits but it grieved thousands of Indians whom the "Black Fathers" had protected and served. It was a costly act, which deprived the Spanish colonies of their best teachers and missionaries and it left the Indians in a sullen, disloyal mood.

Great Marian devotions developed in the New World. Shrines to Our Lady were established in nearly all large Catholic centers. The most notable of these was opened at Guadalupe near Mexico City in 1532. Here, on December 9, 1531, a poor Indian boy named Juan Diego was making his way to Mass when he saw a radiant vision of the Blessed Virgin, who told him she wished a shrine built where they stood. To convince the skeptical authorities, she had him bring with him in his mantle some roses which had miraculously bloomed. Juan de Zumarraga, who had arrived in 1528, was Mexico's first archbishop and a firm defender of the Indians. He received Juan Diego's report of the vision. When the boy's mantle was opened by the bishop, all who were present saw an image of the apparition which had appeared on the coarse woven garment. The bishop ordered a shrine built and later a great church was erected. Above its altar is the life-sized image of the apparition imprinted on the cloth mantle—Our Lady of Guadalupe, known in this early period as the Patroness of the Americas. Even today, Our Lady of Guadalupe continues to be the foremost object of Mexico's devotion. December twelfth is the date of the annual fiesta to which Indians from all over Mexico and many tourists come. Even pilgrims from abroad still visit the shrine three miles from Mexico City.

During the revolt against Spain in 1810 Mexican rebels carried the banner of Our Lady of Guadalupe on lances while the loyalists rallied around that of the Virgin of Remedies. The celebrated Virgin of Guadalupe, a statue of unknown origin, shares with the Pillar of Saragossa and the monastery of Montserrat the veneration of Spaniards for Our Lady.

During the seventeenth and eighteenth centuries Spanish and Portuguese control in Latin America declined. The Spanish government in America refused to allow the natives (Criollos) to hold public office and limited their enterprise and trade. In 1760 the Portuguese minister, Pombal, expelled the Jesuits from all Portuguese dominions and in 1767 Charles III suppressed the order in all Spanish lands.

In the Napoleonic wars, revolt brewed in South America, where the Councils refused to recognize Napoleon's brother as king of Spain. In Mexico, in September, 1810, a parish priest, Father Miguel Hidalgo y Costilla, proclaimed the Revolution in the name of Ferdinand VII, the eldest son of King Charles IV (1788-1808). The battle cry throughout Mexico was "Long live Our Lady of Guadalupe."

The war did not end until Spain withdrew its viceroy in 1821. The Central American countries achieved their independence first, while to the South the movement spread rapidly to oust the Spanish from the entire continent. Sixteen republics were formed by people with little experience in government or liberty and in 1822 the United States was the first government in the world to recognize them. The Holy See, influenced by the Holy Alliance, at first considered the new states as rebels. Thus it happened that after the conclusion of the wars of independence, in all Latin America there were hardly any bishops.

But in other respects the religious situation in the new republics began under unfavorable auspices. Most ecclesiastical institutes, especially the higher schools, were ruined. There was a lack of aspirants for the clergy and an educated Catholic laity. Liberal anticlericalism, that disastrous legacy of recent Spanish rule, could freely develop in America, whereas in Europe it was kept for a time within bounds by the reaction in the era of Metternich. In America, the struggle against Church and clergy often appeared as a struggle against Spain and the European system.

It was not until after the mid-nineteenth century that the Holy See was able to conclude concordats with some of the new republics, Costa Rica, Guatemala, Honduras, Nicaragua, El Salvador and Venezuela, where immediately after the signing of the concordat in 1862 a persecution of the Church broke out, and only after 1875 did normal conditions return to that country. In the other republics, the so-called separation of Church and state prevailed. But even where there were concordats, their value was lessened by the unending changes of government and policy.

An age of disorder followed. Leaders who governed despotically were frequently overthrown, exiled or shot. Civil war was not unusual, and while the new governments grappled with conflicting elements on the brink of chaos, the Church suffered greatly in some countries.

Greatest of all, perhaps, was the legal insecurity from which the Church had to suffer in Mexico, which became a republic in 1824. It has been calculated that up to 1876 Mexico changed its constitution thirty-six times and had seventy-two heads of state. The empire of Maximilian of Austria (1864-67), on which Catholics had based high hopes, proved a disappointment, for Maximilian, himself a liberal, was killed after three years. No government was stable until Benito Juarez, who had overthrown the Emperor, seized the capital, and installed himself as the new president. He acted against the Church as a persecutor of the worst sort, inaugurating his anticlerical program in the Constitution of 1857. This provided for the sale of all land held by religious corporations. Juarez' government was overthrown twice, once before and once after the American Civil War, and under the long presidency of Porfirio Diaz, from 1877 to 1911, greater peace was brought to the Church in Mexico, which regained part of its former power. But after Diaz' resignation in 1911 a series of civil wars brought more bloodshed and disorder. Even in the twentieth century severe persecutions erupted again.

In the new Constitution of 1917 the Church was forbidden to conduct primary schools, states were ordered to limit the number of priests, and title to all Church property was to be held by the state. Churches were pillaged, priests persecuted, and a radical labor group seized power. They wanted complete destruction of the Church. The hierarchy in Mexico refused to recognize the anticlerical articles in the Constitution of 1917. Then all Catholic schools and convents were closed and all priests were required to register with the government. Small armed bands rose under the banner of Christ the King. These forces were routed; many Catholics were executed, including Father Miguel Pro, in November, 1926. It was not until 1940, when Avila Camacho was elected president for six years, that the outlook for religion became brighter and the government more lenient toward the Church in Mexico.

XXX

The Catholic Church
in the Twentieth Century

The twentieth century dawned on a strong Catholic Church still under the firm hand and guidance of Leo XIII, who was to reign as Pontiff until 1903. In spite of the turmoil of the revolutionary period and the anti-clericalism of the nineteenth century the inner structure of the Church had suffered no collapse. Even during the first turbulent thirty years of the twentieth century its basic social structure was to remain unchanged. No one could deny that the prestige of the Church had grown since the close of the nineteenth century.

In France, the book *Du Pape* by Joseph de Maistre did much at the beginning of the nineteenth century to help the revival of papal prestige. The decree of papal infallibility issued at the Vatican Council of 1870 dealt the death blow to Gallicanism. More and more after that, the Papacy adopted the policy of concordats. Throughout the century it showed itself willing to make any possible concessions to national desires in order to secure circumstances favorable to the Church's spiritual activities and growth. The development of a supposed hostility between science and religion was one feature of the nineteenth-century struggle and led some to regard the Papacy as obscurantist and out of date. But the Papacy steadily made gains. The papal declaration of infallibility came at a good time, when this clear, courageous statement was needed. The Papacy was now able to disentangle itself from the complex and sometimes sordid politics of Europe. By means of its spiritual authority the Papacy commanded the obedience of men and attained the great position it held when the twentieth century opened.

That very year of the Vatican Council, 1870, saw Italian nationalism under the House of Savoy deprive the Papacy of its temporal authority in Italy. Not until 1929 was the Lateran Treaty signed between the Holy See and the Kingdom of Italy, creating the Vatican City State over which the Pope exercises spiritual and temporal authority. Until this time he had been "the prisoner of the Vatican." This delimitation in no real sense lessened papal authority. Rather, from thence papal prestige has increased. Many states which had rejected papal claims in the past secured representation to the Vatican. The Church has found it necessary to cope with many states that she might be free to carry out her obligations in the spiritual sphere.

By way of contrast, after the death of Pius IX in 1878 occurred that shameful incident when a Roman mob, stirred up by anticlericals, hurled insults at the Pope's coffin as it was taken through the streets of the city at night. Mud was thrown at the funeral cortege and there was an attempt to seize the Pope's body and throw it into the Tiber River. When Pius' successor, Leo XIII, died in 1903, there was universal expression of sympathy and respect. This was a hopeful sign for the Church in the early years of a century which has turned out, however, to be a century of troubles.

The successor of Leo XIII was Giuseppe Sarto, patriarch of Venice. This son of a peasant family from northern Italy was neither politician, philosopher nor scholar but he was in the truest sense pastor of his flock, guardian of its faith and morals, reformer, and he is now honored as St. Pius X (1903-14). The work of his reign was at once constructive and practical. No Pope since the Council of Trent brought about so many changes, much needed and important, in Catholic life. He promoted frequent reception of the Blessed Sacrament and the early reception of the Eucharist by children. These two decrees revolutionized Catholic piety. Through another papal decree, *Motu proprio,* Pius X restored the music known as Gregorian Plain Chant to a position of primacy in all sacred ceremonies and he made the scientific researches of the Benedictine monks of Solesmes the foundation of the chant's official version. The Pontifical Institute of Sacred Music was established in Rome with the power to grant degrees in sacred music. Later the Pius X School of Liturgical Music was established at Manhattanville College of the Sacred Heart in New York City with similar degree-granting powers.

Pius X revised the calendar of feasts, restored the cycle of Sunday offices and transformed the Divine Office (the daily prayers recited by all priests and many religious). The offices and duties of the Roman curia were rearranged and its procedures reorganized. Many improvements were made in the seminaries of Italy, encouragement was given to the revival of Thomist studies and a commission given to Benedictine scholars to restore the authentic text of St. Jerome's Latin translation of Sacred Scripture. The greatest reform of all was the recodification of Canon Law. The new *Codex* was published in 1917.

In the early years of Pius X's pontificate a bitter persecution of the Church was under way in France. In 1905 the anti-Catholic government separated the Church completely from the state, and passed laws or-

dering the expulsion of all religious orders, the confiscation of their property and the seizure of all Catholic
schools and institutions. Who would now own and administer the former ecclesiastical property? The state
set up a system of committees *(Associations Culturelles)*
as the new owners. Pius X condemned the entire system.
French Catholics were forbidden to have any part in
the arrangement, and they obeyed the order unanimously. The crisis proved the essential quality and sol-
idarity of French Catholicism.

The new German Emperor, Wilhelm II (1888-
1918), who had dismissed Bismarck as Chancellor soon
after he assumed the crown, courted the favor of Rome.
He even visited the Vatican, permitted the reopening of
the seminaries in Germany and allowed the return of
several religious orders. It was during the pontificate of
Pius X, however, that a new conflict arose between the
Church and the German government. The heresy
known as Modernism attempted to make Catholicism
reconcilable to the scientific thought of the day by re-
pudiating the Church's objective supernatural character,
reducing the Catholic Faith to a matter of individual
religious psychology. Modernism was condemned in the
papal encyclical *Pascendi Dominici Gregis* (1907). The
papal pronouncement required priests and teachers of
the Church to take an oath against Modernism. Fearing
an invasion of what it considered its authority over
education, the German government protested against
the oath. In a letter to the German prelates (1910), the
Pope promised that the oath would be restricted to
priest-professors engaged in purely ecclesiastical functions. Many Protestants and even some Catholics
thought that Pius X was severe, even ruthless in his condemnation of Modernism and in the disciplinary steps
he took, but as the Protestant Dean Inge has pointed

out, the Pope could not logically do otherwise than ban a system of thought which undermined the whole fabric of Catholic belief.[83]

Despite remnants of the *Kulturkampf* which remained in force until after World War I, Catholicism increased steadily in numbers, organization and publications in Germany. One evidence of the growing strength of the Church was the continued contributions of German Catholics to modern historical scholarship.

In 1911, an event which went unnoticed but which was to have significant results was the beginning of operations by the Catholic Foreign Mission Society of America, known generally as the Maryknoll Fathers. Seven years later the first trained missionaries were sent to the Far East. These priests and a similar foundation of Sisters have been departing from the Hudson River site's Mother House to fields afar ever since, forming one of America's best-known contributions to the missionary effort. Already they have given more than their share of martyrs and confessors of the Faith in Communist China, a blood-stained field cultivated by the work of such noble representatives of the apostolate as Bishop Ford.

The last illness of Pius X in the late summer of 1914 was hastened by the sorrow and shock he suffered when war broke out August 4. His successor was Benedict XV (1914-22), the learned Genoese cardinal who had been Bishop of Bologna. During his short reign all his energies were devoted to works of charity and peace. In the international quarrel he kept a scrupulous neutrality, while protesting whenever acts occurred which were a breach of moral law. Equal charity was shown to all the victims of war. The Pope took every opportunity to suggest a truce. Twice he made strenuous efforts to end the tragedy by pleading with the belligerents for a truce; his diplomatic note of August 1, 1917 contained his peace proposals, but on both occasions his efforts were repudiated first by the Allies, and then by the Central Powers.

More successful was the humanitarian work of the Papacy both during and after the Great War. Alms on a truly magnificent scale, considering the Pope's resources, went to the countries devastated by the German occupation during the war, and afterward to Russia and to the starving people and children of Central Europe. A principal instrument of papal work was the Prisoners of War Bureau set up at the Vatican in December, 1914, as a means of communication and succor for war prisoners and their families. During the war Pope Benedict gave away five and a half million lire from his own purse and some thirty millions more contributed by Catholics in the churches that could be reached by the Papacy. Later even larger sums of money and the labor of many volunteer workers were devoted to the relief of the suffering caused by war.

The death of a saint usually goes unnoticed—even by Catholics—until canonization brings the saint to public notice. So it was with Mother Francis Xavier Cabrini, who founded an Italian congregation of nuns for work among the poor, known as the Missionary Sisters of the Sacred Heart. In 1889 she led the first group of her nuns out of Europe to America to work among the poor in schools, hospitals and orphanages. Some months after war came to America she died in New York City in December, 1917. Mother Cabrini was destined to become the first American citizen to be elevated to sainthood.

The policy of the three pontificates since 1914 has shown a continuity rare in papal history. This has been due first to the unusual circumstance that the newly

elected Pius XI (1922-39) in 1922 retained in his office
the cardinal who had been since 1914 Benedict XV's
Secretary of State, Pietro Gasparri; and then, Pope Pius
XI appointed his own pupil, Eugenio Pacelli, to suc-
ceed Gasparri; and finally, on the death of Pius XI,
Cardinal Pacelli was himself elected Pope, as Pius XII.

One of the most vexatious problems in the postwar
era was the continuance of "the Roman question," that
is, the position of the Pope as "prisoner of the Vatican."
During all the time this situation existed, state visits to
the King of Italy were regarded, according to existing
papal protocol, as an affront to the Vatican. The French
President, in 1904, ignored this protocol which was
binding on the heads of Catholic states and paid a state
visit to the Italian King in Rome. The Pope protested
and bitter recriminations followed in France. In 1929
Pius XI brought an end to this situation. His Secretary
of State, Cardinal Gasparri, signed the Lateran Treaty
with Italian Premier Benito Mussolini. This accord
established permanent relations between the Papacy and
the Italian state. The small municipality, Vatican City,
with its 108 acres was recognized by Italy and the
world as a sovereign state. A payment of indemnities
to the Papacy by Italy was also agreed on.[84] As Denis
Meadows has written:

> The settlement was a statesmanlike move from
> which the Church reaped the benefit in dealing with
> Italy herself and in easier contact with other gov-
> ernments. The treaty was not, as might have been
> feared by some people, a "deal" with Fascismo.
> Mussolini, of course, welcomed an arrangement
> that added to his prestige with a Catholic popula-
> tion, but he was too shrewd to demand any recog-
> nition by the pope of a totalitarian régime; this

would have wrecked the success of the negotiations and weakened his position with Catholics generally.[85]

There was also a religious part of the agreement between the Holy See and the Italian state that liberated the Church in Italy from the yoke it had borne for centuries. For Pius XI the Treaty's main importance was "the giving back of Italy to God." For the first time in hundreds of years the Pope could appoint bishops to all the sees of Italy without interference from civil power, and the teaching of religion once more entered Italian education. After a century of antireligious violence, Catholicism in Italy at last gained legal recognition of its most elementary rights.

One of the Pope's major problems was to formulate with the new states of Europe treaties which would guarantee Catholics full exercise of their religion. Altogether, a series of twelve concordats were negotiated, the most famous of which was with the German Reich (signed September 18, 1933), and destined to be flouted openly by the Nazis before the ink was dry. In France the national peril of the years after 1914 weakened the remaining anticlericalism; diplomatic relations with the Holy See were resumed and in 1924 Pius XI was successful in negotiating a French settlement on ecclesiastical property through a new system of *Associations Culturelles* in which the Church was now officially represented.

The pontificate of Pius XII (1939-58) came during one of the most trying periods of all church history. Bishop Fulton J. Sheen, who is a student of that history, likens the trying periods through which the "bark of Peter" has passed to five scourges. These are the persecutions, the Eastern Schism, the Avignon Papacy, the

Protestant revolt and the scourge of Communism. In some respects the years since the end of World War II in 1945 have been the most difficult years of the troubled twentieth century, principally because of the rapid spread of Communism in this period.

Peculiar to Spain, which is unlike other Catholic countries such as France or Italy, is the specially close relationship which persisted between Church and state. As a result, attacks on the state were necessarily attacks on the Church. Social cleavages were also more marked in Spain than elsewhere, and the Church was often involved in almost continuous social strife. Finally, social and economic conditions remained more backward in Spain than in most other countries and the Spanish Church was often accused of being responsible for this backwardness. In such a situation, revolution was endemic. A succession of revolutions was accompanied by the confiscation of Church property, the expulsion of religious orders and the violation of concordats.

Dissension grew steadily in Spain in the 1920's and by 1930 prompted a revolution which sent King Alfonso into exile. A coalition of parties proclaimed the Spanish Republic (1931), and a reign of hostility to the Church was inaugurated with it. Church property was confiscated, clergymen's salaries were discontinued and religious orders were forbidden to teach. In the violence which ensued during 1934 and 1935 many churches were desecrated and burned.

In the elections of 1936, Socialists, leftist Republicans, Communists and anarchists, referred to collectively as the Popular Front or the Loyalists, secured the balance of power and determined to stamp out conservative and Catholic opposition. The conservative opposition (the Nationalists), including the army, rose up in July, 1936, under the leadership of Generalissimo Francisco Franco to destroy the Loyalists' government, and civil war ensued. Communist Russia sent men and arms to aid the Loyalists, while Fascist Italy and Germany backed Franco's forces.

Before the bloody war in Spain was over, an estimated thirty thousand priests and nuns were killed, hundreds of convents destroyed and numerous churches desecrated. A skillful propaganda, Communist-inspired, led much of the world to regard the Loyalists, who were responsible for much of this destruction, as defenders of Spanish democracy, and, since their defeat, as martyrs. However, there was less cause for satisfaction over the Spanish Nationalists' victory than some Catholics imagined. As was to be expected, it was followed by a dictatorship and the Papacy had learned, out of hard experience, that dictators, if possible, often use the Church rather than serve her. Moreover, while the atrocities committed against Catholic priests and religious were many and abominable, atrocities were not limited to the Republican side. Even Catholics, if they were well informed, could not be blind to the horrors inflicted on the intensely Catholic, but Republican, Basques.[86] Most Catholics, however, desired a Nationalist victory and their desires were fulfilled when Madrid fell to Franco's forces in March, 1939. A program of reconstruction was introduced which restored confiscated property and religious education, and brought about a concordat with the Papacy.

In Mussolini's regime, the earliest form of the totalitarian state emerged only a few months after the election of Pius XI (1922-39). From the very beginning, the Pope watched with anxiety the developments in Italy. Many observers were deceived by the Concordat of 1929 into believing that relations between Mussolini's government and the Papacy were cordial and that no dangers needed to be anticipated under a government willing to come to an accommodation on the "Roman question."

Year after year the Pope spoke publicly of the dangers inherent in the theory that the state is omnipotent. And while he spoke, there were repeated governmental measures and attempts to curtail the influence of the Church. In 1931 Mussolini launched an attack on Catholic action in Italy; his troops raided the clubs of the Catholic Youth Movement and beat up all the personnel they could lay hands on.[87] With this, the storm of antagonism between Church and state burst in all its fury. The Pope condemned the efforts by the state to infringe on the spheres of the Church. In his letter, *Non Abbiamo Bisogno* (June 29, 1931), he denounced the Fascist ideology as a "real pagan worship of the state," incompatible with Catholic doctrine; he thus made clear that no Catholic could be a genuine Fascist. There was no reply to Pius XI by the Italian government but later the seized property was restored, the Fascists behaved more reasonably toward the Church, and an uneasy truce followed.

In Hitler's Germany, after 1933 there was no longer even a pretense of a truce or an official neutrality regarding the Church and clergy, whether Protestant or Catholic. After Hitler became Chancellor, a slow, steady suppression of Catholicism and persecution of Catholics began. Almost all Catholic organizations and associations were dissolved or brought under the party's heel. National Socialism, which was at first only a political movement, became a religion. The Nazi propaganda machine, masterminded by Joseph Goebbels, went into high gear, fanning German anticlericalism to a white heat. Absurd charges of immorality were brought against nuns and priests and the ensuing trials were given the widest publicity. Church property was confiscated and any affiliations religious orders had outside Germany were cut off. Eventually Germany was so completely closed off from the outside world that the opinion persisted in Catholic lands that no persecution of the Church was really under way in Nazi Germany. Actually, however, scores of nuns and priests were convicted in mock trials, on the most varied of accusations, or even without any, and were thrown into concentration camps. In 1945, when Allied armies liberated these victims of the concentration camps, nearly two thousand priests were found among the prisoners of Dachau alone. During the period of internment, for some of them since before the outbreak of the war, they had suffered untold agonies, since the S.S. guards took special glee in torturing men of God. Apparently one of Heinrich Himmler's obsessions was a pathological hatred of Catholics, whom he had sworn to exterminate along with the Jews.

Imprisonment of Catholic priests and nuns often came as the result of sheltering or aiding the victims of anti-Jewish persecution. In one case, two hundred Jews awaiting betrayal to the Gestapo, the prelude to extermination, were saved by the personal intervention of Pius XII, who handed over a large sum in gold to buy the release of these Jewish prisoners. When Mussolini aped Hitler's scourge of the Jews, many more clerics were victimized for helping them. The patient Pope was sorely tried after five years of Nazi violations, not only of the Concordat but of the laws of humanity. Finally patient diplomacy came to an end with the papal encyclical *Mit Brennender Sorge* ("With Burning Anxiety"), of March 14, 1937, which had to be smuggled into Germany in order to be read from pulpits of the country by courageous clergymen who risked everything in reading it. Pius XI exposed "with shattering force" the Nazi mixture of fraud and cruelty and denounced the whole concept of Nazism as contrary to Christian principles.

When World War II threatened, Pius XII did what he could to work for peace. When hostilities broke out, his efforts were concentrated on works of mercy. The Vatican eventually became a great relief station—the refuge for the fugitives, the stateless and the destitute of all warring nations.

Active resistance by Catholics to Nazism in Germany, or to Fascism in Italy for that matter, as indeed any opposition by the people in an armed state, was suicidal. All legal channels were blocked. In Germany numerous notes and protests were registered by ecclesiastical authorities but they were swallowed up, unanswered, in the massive office bureaucracy Nazism created. "Thus," writes the German church historian, Father Ludwig Hertling, "nothing was left, as in all real persecutions, except to hold out, to preserve what there was to preserve, and for the rest to hope that the storm would not last too long." [88]

Fascism in Italy and Nazism in Germany were merely milder varieties of totalitarianism when compared with the higher fulfillment this system of state supremacy reached in Russian Communism. For all the reasons Fascism was later condemned, Communism too was condemned as far back as 1878 by Pope Leo XIII. Long before the Communist triumph in the Revolution of 1917, throughout the nineteenth century the Russian Empire had been hostile to Catholics. The Tzars had persecuted their Polish subjects, the few Russians who were Catholics, and above all Russian Catholics who followed the Greek liturgy but were in union with Rome.

In the period following World War I, after the whole world had witnessed the triumph of the Soviets, new persecutions began, not only of Catholics but of all religions. All Church property was forfeited to the government without compensation; monasteries were abolished; large numbers of churches were forced to close along with seminaries. The League of Militant Atheists was organized to carry out antireligious propaganda. Protests against these acts were repeated by the Papacy, which ordered prayers to be said for Russia at the end of every Mass offered every day in Catholic churches throughout the world. Finally, in 1937 came the encyclical of Pius XI on atheistic Communism.

More forceful than papal condemnation was the deeply religious nature of the Russian people. While state education rendered godless a large element in the population, many more Russians remained Christian. They effectively hindered the antireligious policy of the Communist regime, which finally modified its religious policy in the face of this passive resistance.

Around 1939 the Soviet government inaugurated a new religious policy representing a gradual retreat from previous extremist antireligious measures. By 1943-44 religion was readmitted into public life, seminaries were reopened and organs of government-controlled propaganda even conceded that Christianity had made a great cultural contribution to Russia's past. Undoubtedly, this degree of religious toleration by the Russian government was designed to strengthen the power of the state, especially as the war with Nazi Germany worsened and strained every available resource.

Withal, there was no concrete regularization or encouragement of the status of the Roman Catholic

Church in Russia. This problem grew more acute when, after World War II, Communism began to spread rapidly in areas outside Russia. The Soviet Union had come to exemplify fully two of the most common features of totalitarianism: dictatorship at home and an aggressive foreign policy. Accordingly, not only has the Soviet Union absorbed a number of neighboring countries of Europe since the war, or aided in placing Communist regimes in control, but the Communist Party has made startling gains in countries of Western Europe (such as Italy and France) and in Asia and Africa. Even traditionally Catholic Cuba in the Western Hemisphere has shown itself to be vulnerable to "peaceful penetration" by the Communists. About one-third of the world's population is now under Communist domination. With Russian rule or influence over so many Catholics today, as in Eastern Europe, there is an urgent need for some granting of religious freedom for the Russian Orthodox Church as well as for the Catholic and Uniate Churches. But there is less cause today for optimism than at any earlier time since the complete separation of the Russian state from the Church in 1918.

In those lands only recently subjected to Russian rule the Catholic Church has suffered in varying degrees. Modern martyrs to Russian tyranny are more numerous than the record indicates. In 1946 Archbishop Stepinac of Zagreb in Yugoslavia was tried and condemned to sixteen years' imprisonment. He died while under house arrest. In 1949 occurred the even more sensational trial and imprisonment of Hungary's primate, Joseph Cardinal Mindszenty. Archbishop Beran of Prague was forcibly removed from office by the government and since his banishment nothing certain is known of his whereabouts. These are but a few examples of the many champions of the Faith who have preferred death or prison to the ungodly principles of an armed state.

The Communist victory in China in 1949 resulted in the expulsion or imprisonment of all foreign-born missionaries and the imprisonment or death of all native priests and nuns. Doubtless, the Church has had many more martyrs in Communist China than the world has come to know.

Many features of twentieth-century life and certain present-day tendencies give pause—and may even prompt pessimism and near despair. Millions throughout the world today are devoted, militant, even fanatical believers in Marxism. Vast areas are firmly under totalitarian governments, and in view of the technical and economic achievements of Soviet Russia, the Church of St. Peter is now face to face with an enemy of incalculable power and determination. Stalin once asked, contemptuously, "How many divisions can the Pope put in the field?" The answer, of course, is not a single one—and moreover, the Papacy has explicitly vetoed the idea of an armed "crusade" against the Communist world, even if such an idea were practicable.[89]

We note, however, that Communist parties and governments pay Catholicism the tribute of hating it; they are not so stupid as to ignore it. Indeed, it would be hard to ignore the fact that as we near the closing decades of the twentieth century the number of Catholics throughout the world approaches 450 million. In the Church there is a higher level of religious devotion and practice than ever before. Prevailing standards of priestly and monastic life are also higher than ever before.

The century has seen one of the most remarkable successions of Pontiffs in the Church's long history. One of them, Pius X, was canonized a saint in 1954. And when the respected religious leader, Pius XII, died in 1958, a universal wave of popular sympathy swept over the world, touching millions outside the Church over which he had ruled so wisely and well. A similarly genuine affection and regard for Pope John XXIII, the former Cardinal Roncalli, Patriarch of Venice, chosen as his successor, augurs well for the success of the ambitious projects he has set up. His decision to convene a twenty-first Ecumenical Council has been well received. Through it he wishes to make approaches to the various bodies of separated Christians, starting with the Eastern Orthodox Churches. A recent meeting of Pope John with the Archbishop of Canterbury—the first in five hundred years—distinguishes his pontificate even in its early years for its broad-mindedness and its desire to seek common Christian grounds upon which challenges from anti-Christian forces can be met and overcome.

By far the greatest task confronting the Catholic Church today is the recovery to the Faith of the millions who are now nominally Marxist believers. A mighty ideological struggle has built up between the forces of irreligious collectivism and essentially God-fearing nations devoted to principles of freedom and individualism. The secularism of these nonreligious peoples has driven religious leaders of all faiths closer together, and discussion continues about the possibility of some Protestant groups returning to the Catholic Church. Whether the society of the future will be dominated by irreligious and Communistic principles or whether these forces will be subdued, inaugurating a new religious Golden Age, depends on Divine Providence. Catholics, however, believe that whatever happens, their Church cannot suffer extinction.

Notes

1. Preserved Smith, *The Age of the Reformation.*

2. Denis Meadows, *A Short History of the Catholic Church,* p. 2.

3. Meadows, *op. cit.,* p. 3.

4. Meadows, *op. cit.,* pp. 11-12.

5. Meadows, *op. cit.,* pp. 14-15.

6. Meadows, *op. cit.,* p. 18.

7. Meadows, *op. cit.,* p. 48.

8. Meadows, *op. cit.,* p. 49.

9. Philip Hughes, *A Popular History of the Catholic Church,* p. 68.

10. Ludwig Hertling S. J., *A History of the Catholic Church,* p. 169.

11. Martin E. Marty, *A Short History of Christianity,* p. 101.

12. Hughes, *op. cit.,* p. 89.

13. In token of this Cluny was to pay a feudal tax of five gold pieces every fifth year for the maintenance of the lamps that burned before the tombs of the apostles in Rome. Hertling, *op. cit.,* p. 191.

14. Pope Nicholas I had excommunicated King Lothair of Lorraine because he kept the concubine, Waldrada, and no one disputed the Pope's right to do this. Hertling, *op. cit.,* p. 213.

15. "The Twelfth Century: the Flowering of the Middle Ages," *Jubilee* Magazine (May, 1959), pp. 27-37.

16. Bernard Myers, *Art and Civilization,* p. 298.

17. *Ibid.,* pp. 311ff.

18. Mosaic art is a form of painting with myriads of colored stones and bits of glass.

19. "The Twelfth Century: the Flowering of the Middle Ages," in *Jubilee* Magazine (May, 1959), p. 33.

20. At the Third Lateran Council (1179) the Church ruled that every cathedral church should support a master to

instruct the ecclesiastical students, giving his services free of charge to indigent scholars.

21. Colleges or so-called "burses" were instituted for students in university cities; it was from such a burse, founded by Robert de Sorbon, court chaplain to Saint Louis, that the entire University of Paris was later referred to as the Sorbonne.

22. Hertling, *op cit.*, pp. 237-38; "The Twelfth Century: the Flowering of the Middle Ages," *Jubilee* Magazine (May, 1959), p. 36-37.

23. Thomas P. Neill and Raymond H. Schmandt, *History of the Catholic Church*, pp. 230-31.

24. Hughes, *op. cit.*, p. 117.

25. The Inquisition followed the procedure of the civil courts of that period in admitting anonymous testimony and, for that matter, employing torture.

26. Rev. Anthony J. Flynn, Sister Vincent Loretto, and Mother Mary Simeon, *The Triumph of Faith*, pp. 148-49.

27. Neill and Schmandt, *op. cit.*, p. 232.

28. Quoted in Colman J. Barry, O.S.B., ed., *Readings in Church History*, p. 539.

29. "The Thirteenth: Greatest of Centuries," *Jubilee* Magazine (October, 1959), p. 32.

30. Rev. John K. Cartwright, *The Catholic Shrines of Europe*, pp. 65-66.

31. Hertling, *op. cit.*, p. 245.

32. Hughes, *op. cit.*, p. 127.

33. *Ibid.*

34. *Ibid.*, p. 129.

35. Marty, *op. cit.*, pp. 172-73.

36. George Burch, *Early Medieval Philosophy*, p. 5.

37. Marty, *op. cit.*, p. 174.

38. *Ibid.*

39. Hughes, *op. cit.*, p. 129.

40. Quoted in Anne Freemantle, *The Age of Belief,* p. 148.

41. Marty, *op. cit.*, p. 175.

42. Frederick B. Artz, *The Mind of the Middle Ages*, pp. 380-83.

43. By the medieval interdict is meant a sort of strike on the part of the clergy by order of the Pope. All ecclesiastical rites, including every public divine service excepting the pri-

vate administration of the sacraments of the dying, ceased. Hertling, *op. cit.*, p. 275.

44. Hertling, *op. cit.*, p. 288.

45. Hertling, *op. cit.*, pp. 290-91.

46. Quoted in Hans Kühner, *Encyclopedia of the Papacy*, p. 106.

47. *Op. cit.*, p. 143.

48. *Ibid.*, p. 144.

49. Carlton J. Hayes, Marshall Baldwin, and Charles Cole, *History of Europe*, I, 395.

50. Hughes, *op. cit.*, p. 153.

51. Meadows, *op. cit.*, p. 129.

52. Hughes, *op. cit.*, p. 170.

53. Carlton Hayes, *History of Europe*, p. 469.

54. Quoted by H. S. Lucas in *The Renaissance and the Reformation*, p. 457.

55. Hughes, *op. cit.*, p. 166.

56. Hughes, *op. cit.*, p. 171.

57. Hughes, *op. cit.*, p. 173.

58. Hughes, *op. cit.*, pp. 185-86.

59. Marty, *op. cit.*, pp. 257-58.

60. Theodore Maynard, *The Story of American Catholicism*, pp. 315-16.

61. *Ibid.*, p. 317.

62. "Spain in America," in *Jubilee* Magazine (June, 1955), p. 39.

63. Maynard, *op. cit.*, p. 47.

64. Herbert Bolton, *The Rim of Christendom*, p. 4.

65. W. H. Browne, *Archives of Maryland*, I, 244-47.

66. "First Martyr from the New World," in *Maryknoll* (November, 1958), p. 63.

67. Meadows, *op. cit.*, pp. 192-94.

68. Meadows, *op. cit.*, p. 180.

69. Neill and Schmandt, *op. cit.*, p. 435.

70. Hughes, *op. cit.*, p. 235.

71. Meadows, *op. cit.*, p. 198.

72. Meadows, *op. cit.*, p. 200.

73. Marty, *op. cit.*, p. 280.

74. *Ibid.*, pp. 280-81.

75. Hertling, *op. cit.*, p. 531.
76. Hughes, *op. cit.*, p. 234.
77. *Op. cit.*, pp. 228-29.
78. *Ibid.*
79. *Ibid.*, p. 255.
80. Neill and Schmandt, *op. cit.*, pp. 552-53.
81. Meadows, *op. cit.*, pp. 216-17.
82. Hughes, *op. cit.*, p. 267; Meadows, *op. cit.*, p. 217.
83. Meadows, *op. cit.*, pp. 220-21.
84. Meadows, *op. cit.*, pp. 225-26.
85. *Ibid.*
86. *Ibid.*, pp. 227-28.
87. Hughes, *op. cit.*, p. 276.
88. *Op. cit.*, p. 571.
89. Meadows, *op. cit.*, p. 235.

Index

DATE DUE